LEARN TO LOVE YOURSELF AGAIN IN 7 DAYS

How to Stop Negative Self Talk and Start Taking Control of Life, Including 40+ Love Yourself Quotes for Boosting Self Esteem

SOPHIE DAWSON

TABLE OF CONTENTS

INTRODUCTION

You've grown up and left high school behind you. You're an adult. You shouldn't feel jealous of people you went to school with years ago. But as soon as you go on social media, you're bombarded with pictures of your peers leading extraordinary lives. They've got high paid jobs, or they're vacationing in exotic locations and you're left feeling like a failure. Does that sound familiar? Well, guess what? Everyone has probably felt this way at one time or another. But what about the happy smiling photos of your friends wearing designer clothes and looking successful? Those aren't a real representation of their day to day existence. The pictures people post of themselves on social media are posed and don't represent everyday life. The well-put-together school chum holding a smiling toddler may not have had a decent night of sleep for months and they may be holding onto their sanity by a thread. The first step in learning how to love yourself is to stop comparing yourself to others. This might sound almost impossible, but we'll teach you how.

It's not just social media that can make you feel like a failure. Do you feel like you aren't getting anywhere in life? Are you stuck in a dead-end job? Or do you find yourself going for job interview after job interview and getting nowhere? It all might seem to point to one thing: that you're not good enough. But this isn't true! You are good enough. You just have to believe it. But how can you believe you're good enough when all the evidence seems to prove otherwise?

There's one trick to doing well in life: love. We all want to be loved. Human beings are hardwired to seek out love. We all dream of one day finding 'the one', that special individual to love unconditionally. But there's one person we often forget to love: ourselves. You can't love anyone else until you've learned to love yourself. Loving yourself means more than just thinking about yourself. It means treating yourself with compassion. When we give ourselves the compassion to forgive past mistakes and take time to ensure we care for ourselves, we become more successful. Self-compassion means replacing negative self-talk with a positive outlook. Positivity can help us achieve our goals, and reach for heights we've never imagined.

In this book, we'll teach you how to turn your back on negative self-talk and overcome self-doubt in order to become confident and successful. You'll learn that it's okay to celebrate your victories in order to spur you on to even greater achievements. Your confidence will grow to the point where you will not only accept failures, but appreciate them for what they can teach you. Many things from your past can hold you back and keep you from being your true, successful self. You will learn how to let go of the past, forgive yourself for your mistakes and ultimately understand what it means to love yourself.

It doesn't matter how positive or confident you are, if your environment is holding you back, you won't be free to succeed. We'll show you how to create an environment in which you thrive. You won't have to worry about the negativity of the people and places that stop you from being everything you're meant to be. You can learn to put self-compassion into practice every day, and you'll be transformed once you learn how to treat yourself with the love you deserve. Then you can move on to take control of your life and be your best self.

Once you've learned how to love yourself, we'll take you through 10 mindfulness meditations to truly clear your thoughts and give yourself the deep, restful peace that will help shed your anxiety and put you at your best. Moreover, 40+ 'loving yourself' quotes will motivate you to foster the love you deserve every single day so that you have the strength, self-compassion and confidence to achieve all of your goals.

By reading just 2 chapters a day, you can gain all the knowledge and power you need to become more positive and focused on how to thrive, succeed and be happy. In 7 days, you really can learn all the skills for how to love yourself, be confident about who you are and take control of where your life is heading, after all, you deserve it.

CHAPTER ONE

WHAT IS NEGATIVE SELF-TALK AND WHY IS IT HARMFUL?

Give your inner voice the power to lift you up. Make words
of love the gift you give yourself every day.

There's a job you've always dreamed of applying for. You've got the training and the experience for it. It would be perfect for you; you know you can do it and do it well. But then the doubts start to creep in. As you fill out the application, a voice in your head whispers that you might not actually be that experienced. You've only been in your current job a few years, after all. And your training was so many years ago, what you learned back then can't possibly be relevant today. The employer is sure to want someone younger with modern, up-to-date training. You know you're good at your current job…but are you *really?*

As you try to think of something positive to say about your abilities your mind goes blank. All you can think about are the negative things: you're not fast enough, you make too many mistakes, and people don't like you. You stare blankly at the application form. The job is a huge step up. You wonder how you could possibly perform well when you can't even manage the job you've already got. You fold the application form in half and throw it into the rubbish. You wonder what you were even thinking? You shake your head. *That job is way too good for me,* you decide. You try to tell yourself that you should be happy with the job you already have, but there's a feeling of longing inside you. You stare wistfully at the job application in the rubbish bin. *Could I?* you wonder, and you hastily push the question down. *No,* you tell yourself. *No, I can't.*

Does this sound familiar? This is negative self-talk in action. Negative self-talk occurs when our inner voices are far too critical of us, making us view the world and ourselves in a negative light. Sometimes it's helpful to think critically about things. For instance, telling ourselves it's best not to eat a second piece of chocolate cake because too much sugar might not be good for us is constructive; it's important to look after our health and we may come to regret overeating. However, when our self-criticism becomes less constructive and more hypercritical, it can do you more harm than good. When our self-evaluation goes too far, it turns into negative self-talk.

10 TYPES OF NEGATIVE SELF-TALK

According to the Harvard University Stress and Development Lab, there are 10 kinds of negative self-talk.[1]

---

[1] "Identifying Negative Automatic Thought Patterns," *Stress & Development Lab*, Harvard University, Accessed April 29, 2021. https://sdlab.fas.harvard.edu/cognitive-reappraisal/identifying-negative-automatic-thought-patterns.

1. **Mental Filter:** This type of negative self-talk occurs when people pay too much attention to the negative and ignore the positive. Even if five things went well in a day, the person who is prone to mental filtering will only focus on the one negative thing that happened that day. For instance, you may have had a compliment from your boss on your work ethic, your best friend may have told you looked pretty, you may have managed to run an extra mile that day, you may have reached your savings goal, and you may have been told by another parent that you're doing really well as a mother and that your child/children have perfect manners.

   That all sounds like a perfectly wonderful day, a day to be proud of. Except if you have mental filtering, you won't see it that way. Let's say something not so good happened that day. You may have had an angry client at work. They may have been dissatisfied and asked to see the boss. Instead of seeing this as a minor blip in an otherwise excellent day, mental filtering may make you see it as the *only* thing of consequence that happened that day. The truth is the client may have been upset at the rules of the workplace. These rules may have been beyond your control. In other words, they had nothing to do with you. The client may have had a bad day. Some people know that they can get what they want if they only complain loudly enough. Above all, as most people who have worked in customer service can attest, it's most unlikely that the client's response is your fault. Disgruntled clients are sometimes just part of the job. Yet, if you have mental filtering, you may believe the client's annoyance is solely your fault. You may judge yourself as letting the client down, or not being skilled enough to talk them around.

2. **All-or-nothing Thinking:** This type of thinking allows for no gray areas. Everything is black and white. Good or bad. Phrases like "always" or "never" become the norm. An example of all-or-nothing negative self-talk would be, "I will always fail," "I will never be popular," "My boss will never give me a promotion," or "I will never be good at anything." All-or-nothing thinking can make things seem worse than they are, and stressful situations can be blown out of proportion or completely misinterpreted.

3. **Disqualifying the Positive:** Positive experiences are treated like happenstance by people who debunk the positive. Debunking the positive leads to having low expectations for the future and there's a tendency to foresee negative outcomes. When having the positives pointed out to them, people who debunk the positive will likely respond with "yes, but," or "maybe, except."

4. **Overgeneralization:** Negative self-talk that involves overgeneralization means people will look at a situation and see all future instances of that situation in the same way. For example, an individual may experience a taxi driver who purposefully takes the long route and drives extra slowly to up the fare. An overgeneralizer may then conclude that all taxi

drivers are crooks who want to cheat their customers into an inflated fare.

5. **Emotional Reasoning:** Certain truths are ignored when making conclusions during emotional reasoning. People will judge a situation by their emotions rather than the facts in emotional reasoning. For instance, the emotion may be anger at something another person has done. The conclusion during emotional reasoning would be to blame the other person for the emotion of anger, even though it may or may not be their fault that you're angry.

6. **Personalization:** The negative self-talker blames them self when things go wrong. When negative experiences happen that a person has no control over, blaming oneself causes a lot of unnecessary stress. For instance, if a customer is unhappy, causing them to walk out so you lose a sale, try not to take it personally. They could have been having a bad day. Or they may have had higher expectations of the product or service they were interested in. Most likely, nothing you could have done would change the outcome.

7. **Labelling and Mislabelling:** Labelling in negative self-talk means someone will label themselves in negative ways. For instance, they might call themselves "a useless moaner," "a failure as a mother," or "a boring loner."

8. **Magnifying and Minimizing:** This is when an individual may see their failures as far more momentous than they are, and

they drastically downplay their achievements. This goes beyond politeness or trying to appear humble. The individual will believe their achievements are nothing. For example, a salesperson who downplays meeting their target by saying that the demand is strong for the product is minimizing their part in the positive outcome.

9. **Jumping to Conclusions**: Negative self-talk can make you jump to the wrong conclusions. You may have a negative conclusion pre-formed in your head that will distort how you perceive an event. You will look for evidence to back up your wrong conclusion and ignore evidence that contradicts it. For instance, if your friend doesn't answer your call straight away despite saying they are busy, you might immediately assume they don't like you anymore.

10. **Should Statements**: When you use "should" or "shouldn't" statements about how you act or feel, this can lead to guilt if you are too harsh on yourself. For instance, "I shouldn't be so silly" or "I should try to be more interesting."

WHY NEGATIVE SELF-TALK IS SO HARMFUL

Negative self-talk doesn't just stay in your mind. It has a huge effect on your everyday life. It can stop you from doing the things you want to do. For instance, you may find yourself in a relationship that is not good for you. You know you should probably leave the relationship for your own self-esteem or happiness, yet your negative self-talk prevents you from leaving the unhealthy relationship. Some of the things your inner-voice might say include "I'll never find anyone else who will love me," "It's my fault they treat me badly. I deserve it," or "I'll never cope on my own." This kind of negative self-talk can lead people to stay in relationships that aren't just bad for them, but that might be frightening or even dangerous situations. Negative self-talk can be so strong, it can prevent us from taking the steps we need to in order to keep ourselves healthy or safe.

Negative self-talk can stop you from reaching your potential. Have you ever avoided the chance to better yourself out of fear of failure? Did you want to apply for a raise or ask for a promotion at work but you were too afraid to ask because you feared being rejected, or worse, being laughed at or criticised by your boss? This is negative self-talk making you see the worst possible outcome and preventing you from even trying.

Negative self-talk can also lead to mental disorders. When negative self-talk becomes more than just an occasionally critical inner voice, it can start to take over. The more you listen to and act on your negative self-talk, the more it becomes the blueprint for all your thinking. Negative self-talk can lead to mental disorders like depression and anxiety or OCD. It leads to low self-esteem and a general feeling of dissatisfaction or helplessness about your life. It can get in the way of relationships with other people. If your self-esteem is low, you may become needy, wanting lots of attention or constant reassurance from loved ones or friends, which can wear people down. Or if you think you aren't worth loving you may become fearful of your partner leaving you. This could lead to jealousy and overprotectiveness. As your negative self-talk sabotages your thoughts and takes over your life, you may start to lose friends and become lonely. This can lead to feelings of depression. You can become anxious about the need to please people or do well. However, your negative self-talk won't allow you to acknowledge your own success, and no matter how hard you try, you will only continue to doubt yourself and feel worse. Eventually, you may experience anxiety which can manifest itself in many ways, including panic attacks.

All of this may sound familiar. It may also sound scary. If negative self-talk is strong enough to change your thoughts to the point that it gets in the way of your work, your relationships and your mental health, how can you fight it? Don't be afraid. You can fight negative self-talk. Not only that, you can turn it around completely. You can transform negative self-talk into something positive. Your mind is powerful. Your thoughts are powerful. You can use your mind and change your thinking into something good. You can change your life and become whatever you put your mind to. Read on to find out how you can turn your negative thoughts into incredible, positive beliefs.

CHAPTER SUMMARY

In this chapter, you learned…

- Negative self-talk occurs when your inner voice is too critical of you
- Negative self-talk stops you from doing the things you want and prevents you from doing what's best for you
- Negative self-talk can lead to mental disorders like depression and anxiety
- You can change your negative self-talk by turning your thinking into something positive

In the next chapter, you will learn…

- How emotions get in the way of your success and lead to self-doubt
- How to overcome the emotions that lead to self-doubt
- Exercises to help you overcome self-doubt and let you believe in yourself

CHAPTER TWO

OVERCOME SELF-DOUBT AND BELIEVE IN YOURSELF

Your feelings belong to you. Let them guide you.
Let them fill you with the want for a brighter future.
Let them fuel your happiness.

There are a lot of emotions that arise when you face challenges. Sometimes these emotions can get in the way of how you respond to things. Take going for a job interview as an example of a challenging situation. It's understandable to feel nervous when preparing for a job interview. Even the most highly qualified and self-confident person will feel a bit uneasy in this situation. After all, a job is a big part of your life. It will determine where you go and what you do almost every day. It will affect your income and lifestyle. A little bit of excitement and adrenaline can help you in these situations by making you alert and quick thinking. It's when your emotions take over that it becomes a problem. When nerves take over you won't be able to think clearly. You might start to sweat, which can make you feel self-conscious, only adding to your nervousness. If your emotions really take over, you could start to panic. Panic is what happens when your emotions cause you to go into fight or flight mode. In dangerous situations, fight or flight mode can mean the difference between life or death. In a job interview…it's not so helpful. You won't be able to think clearly, you may not be able to concentrate on the questions you're being asked. If you've been through a job interview like this before, you'll probably never want to apply for another job again! And who would blame you? But it doesn't have to be this way. You can overcome your emotions and self-doubt in order to succeed.

Try to think of the emotions you feel when you face a situation where you doubt yourself. If you have difficulty thinking of the emotion right now, don't worry, it can be hard to know what you're feeling when you're in a tough situation. Some of these emotions may include feeling stressed or anxious, you might feel annoyed because you don't want to face a certain situation, you may even feel sad or helpless. Next time you're in a situation where self-doubt overcomes you, try to identify the emotion you experienced at the time. If you're unsure, try to think of what happened to your body when you were in a challenging situation. Did your heart race? Did you start to sweat? Did your mouth go dry? Did you find yourself stuttering? These are all signs of anxiety, stress or nervousness.

It may seem like the emotions you feel are overwhelming and that you'll never be able to change them. But you can. Take the example of how to overcome extreme nervousness when going for a job interview. In this instance, the emotion of self-doubt leads to anxiety, nervousness and self-consciousness. In order to overcome these responses, it's important to acknowledge the emotions. Ignoring them may make you feel better about them, but it can make it difficult to change something if you don't face it. Firstly, know that these feelings don't make you a bad person or a weak person. Feeling nervous is a natural emotion. Everyone experiences this feeling at some time. It's not that you feel nervous that's important, it's how you deal with it. So, as soon as you start to feel the emotion of nervousness, acknowledge it. Be aware that this is an emotion you are feeling but don't allow it to take over. Be aware of your nerves. Understand they are normal human emotions. Try to think of these emotions in a positive light. Nervousness means you are invested in the outcome of what's happening. In this example, it means you're motivated to do well in an interview for a job you may really want. This is a good thing! You have the chance to make your life better. It's exciting! The nerves mean you are facing something important. At this point, you want to stop these nerves from taking over. So, after acknowledging them and trying to think they mean something exciting is about to happen, you have to combat those nerves. You have to find a way to proceed with your interview with confidence. Your nerves shouldn't get in the way of your interview.

There are a number of ways to manage your nervousness. The best way to control your nerves is to take their power away. Tell yourself that your nerves are just a temporary feeling. Whatever emotion accompanies your nerves, panic or fear, for instance, are just feelings. They can't physically hurt you. You *will* be okay. Your nervousness is caused by negative self-talk. So, the second step in shutting it down is to debunk your negative self-talk. If your negative talk says you will fail in your interview, rewrite your mental script. Tell yourself you have prepared for the interview. You have thought about what you will be asked and you should be able to answer most of the questions reasonably well.

Now you're ready to move on to some exercises that you can put into action to help you take back control of your emotions.

1. **Practicing a Positive Mindset**: Learn to focus on the positive and to see the good in everything. If you come across some obstacles, try to flip the script by turning the experience into a positive. For instance, if you are stuck in traffic, try not to get frustrated or focus on how much time you are wasting. Think of it as an opportunity to do something you enjoy. Close your eyes and listen to some music. Take the opportunity to read a book if you have one handy on your device. Or just look at the view and take a moment to enjoy doing nothing. Try to turn a negative situation into a chance for growth or improvement. For example, if you failed your driving test just think about how much easier it will be the next time now you know what to expect.

2. **Breathing Techniques**: Breathing techniques not only make you calm by physically forcing you to focus on your breathing, the process also distracts you from your negative thoughts. This is especially useful in times of stress or negative self-talk. Diaphragmatic breathing is a good technique to begin with. Start by lying on your back with your eyes closed. Place a hand on your chest and the other on your ribcage so you can feel your chest rise and fall. As you breathe in slowly through your

nose, you should feel your stomach rise. By doing so, you are ensuring as much oxygen reaches your lungs as possible. The calming effect of this exercise will help you calm down. In moments when your emotions take over, try this breathing technique in order to calm your thoughts and your breathing. With practice, you should be able to feel when you are starting to become emotional, and you should be able to stop yourself from getting too upset. With this simple step you have already started to take back control of your thoughts and feelings! You have taken the first step in learning to love yourself. Well done!

3. **Meditation:** There's more to meditation than just sitting perfectly still and breathing deeply. In the case of anxiety or nervousness, meditation can allow us to become more aware of the thoughts that cause negative emotions like nervousness. When meditating we understand our emotions, feel and acknowledge them, and then let them go. Meditation encourages practitioners to understand that our thoughts do not define us. Once we separate ourselves from our thoughts we can change our relationship to them. With a more removed, less emotional mindset, we can learn to see the difference between less rational thoughts and more real ones. We can learn to be less hard on ourselves. One of the ways that meditation helps people separate themselves from their emotions is learning how to "be" in the moment. Body awareness is an aspect of meditation, or mindfulness, that allows us to pay attention to the physical things that are

happening. One technique that brings about body awareness is body scanning. To begin this meditation you can sit or lie down somewhere comfortable and close your eyes. Start by feeling the sensation of your toes. If it helps focus you can even curl your toes, in order to concentrate on them more easily. Slowly move up your body scanning the sensations of each part, from your calf muscles, up your thighs, to your hips, your stomach, to your chest, your shoulders, up across your arms, to your neck, go through the main muscles of your face until you reach the top of your head. The more you practice meditation, the more you will be able to remove yourself from your other thoughts and live in the moment.

4. **Reading Affirmations and Inspiring Quotes:** Instagram poets become famous for a reason. Their words inspire. People have been reaching out to each other with poetry for centuries. Affirmations and inspirational quotes can change our negative thoughts to positive ones. They can even serve as motivation and cause us to put aside our fears and negative self-talk. How is this possible? Affirmations work because our minds can be tricked into thinking the things we imagine are real. For instance, if we imagine ourselves successfully doing something we are afraid of, such as skydiving, the areas of our brains that would activate if we actually did jump out of a plane are activated in the same way. If you repeat positive affirmations to yourself, eventually, our brain takes this as something that's true. So, in the case of preparing for a job interview, if you tell yourself you are relaxed and confident, then it's more likely

that you will be in the real interview, because your brain has already experienced a successful interview! Inspiring quotes work because they appeal to our imagination. Much like affirmations, we imagine ourselves doing whatever the inspiring quotes suggest we do. So, if an inspiring quote tells us to "seize the day," we immediately imagine how we might do that. We picture ourselves making sure we go out and make the absolute most of the day we've been given. Try to do five minutes' worth of affirmations a day and five minutes of reading inspiring quotes.

CHAPTER SUMMARY

In this chapter, you learned...

- Emotions can get in the way of succeeding. For example, fear and anxiety can get in the way during a job interview.
- Overcome these emotions by acknowledging them and taking away their power by debunking your negative self-talk.
- Exercises like breathing exercises and meditation can help you gain control of your emotions when you experience self-doubt.

In the next chapter, you will learn...

- To stop comparing yourself to others
- How to accept your flaws
- How images on social media are distorted
- How to avoid being jealous about what you see on social media

CHAPTER THREE

STOP COMPARING YOURSELF AND STRIVING FOR PERFECTION

No one is perfect. Consider the people you care about the most. Are they perfect? No. Of course not. But do you love them any less? Maybe your mother is a bit of a nag, or maybe your dad chews loudly and eats with his mouth open. Maybe your partner has put on a little weight lately. Do you blame your loved ones for these imperfections? Do you hate them for being less than perfect? Of course, you don't. You accept these imperfections in others and concentrate instead on what you love about them. If we can forgive everyone else for their flaws, why are we so much harder on ourselves?

In order to stop being hard on yourself you need to stop making comparisons. This is more difficult for most of us than it sounds. Society is based on making comparisons. From a young age, we're judged in schools and sports. Even without meaning to, parents judge their children against their siblings. In our workplaces, performance is rewarded based on set goals and comparisons. Right from the moment we learn to talk we are compared to our peers. We're also taught to be modest. We're not meant to talk about our achievements, that would be bragging. Instead, we're taught to downplay our accomplishments. If our parents, teachers and peers admonish us for talking about our success, then we may begin to undervalue our own achievements or brush them aside. We often get a bigger reaction from others for our mistakes than we do for our achievements. We're expected to do well, we're raised and trained to meet certain standards, and when we achieve them we're not often rewarded. Yet, when we fail we tend to get a bigger response from teachers and family. We might be punished, admonished or embarrassed in front of our peers for our mistakes. It's no wonder we tend to put more emphasis on our own failures—this is precisely what society has taught us to do!

So, what can we do to change this overemphasis on the negative? Firstly, we have to accept our flaws. To do that, we need to look a little more closely at these flaws and ask ourselves the following questions:

1. **Is the flaw something I can change?** Some flaws are things we can't change. For instance, you might feel that being too short in stature is a flaw. This is essentially something that we can't do a lot about, so it's not something we can change. Conversely, being a little overweight is something we can change with exercise and healthy eating. Once you've decided whether a flaw is something you can change, you can do something to change it, if you wish. If you can't change the flaw in question, you may need to figure out how to accept it.

2. **Can you accept your flaw?** If a flaw is something we can't change, we need to work on accepting it. Let's consider the

example of being too short in stature as a flaw. If you feel like being too short is a flaw, you need to try to find a way to accept it. Short stature can make certain things in life difficult; it may make it harder for you to find clothes to fit, or you may find it hard to reach things on the shelves in supermarkets. How might you accept this flaw? You might consider whether there are worse flaws you could have. For instance, even though you would like to be taller, you still have your health and the ability to walk. Having to reach up for things may make life more inconvenient, but it's not so terrible. Consider the fact that some people who are tall would wish to be less statuesque. It must be annoying bumping your head on small ceilings and doorways!

3. **Are you being realistic about the flaw?** Sometimes we are hypercritical of ourselves. We may look too closely at the things that we perceive as being imperfect about who we are. For instance, you might think you're not the perfect parent. The funny thing is that this is the way most parents feel. Parenting is hard, and even when someone seems to be coping well, they are probably struggling, too.

Practice the below exercise with any perceived flaws you have that make you worried. You should find that you will either be able to change your flaws, accept them or realize they aren't really flaws at all.

Fill out your own table about accepting your flaws. Here are some examples…

Perceived Flaw	Can it Be Changed? How?	Can I Accept it? How?	Is it really a Flaw?
I'm slightly overweight.	Yes. It can be changed by doing exercise and eating a more balanced and healthy diet.	Yes. I can work on losing weight.	No. I can do something about it.
I'm too quiet.	Yes. I can try to be more outgoing. Maybe I can take a Toastmasters Course to help me learn to speak with confidence.	If I don't manage to become outgoing, I will have to learn to live with the fact that I am not talkative.	No. I think the people who get to know me realize I'm not really boring or antisocial. It just takes me a while to come out of my shell.
I am too short.	No.	I want to be a basketball player. Being short means, I can't achieve my dream. Instead I could try a sport better suited to my body. Such as table tennis.	No. I have to be more realistic about what I am physically able to do.

Eventually, you will reach the point where you can accept your flaws. But what if you reach that point, the point where you are happy with your imperfections, and yet other people's opinions of you don't change? There are always some people in life who will criticize you. If you have realized your flaws aren't so bad, or they are something you should work on, does it matter what other people think? The answer is of course not. Yet, as humans, we are geared from an early age to care about what people think of us. Humans are social creatures. We want to be liked and accepted.

TIPS FOR DEALING WITH NEGATIVE OPINIONS OF YOU

When it comes to criticism, we usually have two immediate responses: we either accept the criticism or we reject it. When we reject criticism, we often take it to heart on some level if only subconsciously. This is where self-doubt can creep in without us even knowing it. A better way to face criticism is to consider it logically without emotion.

The first step in considering criticism is to *listen.* Try to figure out the intention of the critic. Are they coming from a place of destructive intentions or constructive intentions? For example, if a boss derides the work you did on a job without taking the time to look at your work or give an explanation about why your work is subpar, they are not offering constructive criticism. Some people like to criticise in order to feel better about themselves or to feel more powerful or even because they may be jealous. Conversely, if your boss takes the time to explain why your work is not up to par and gives you advice on how to improve you can take this as constructive criticism.

Once you have gauged the intention of the person criticising you, you can then decide what to do about it. If the criticism is constructive and you feel the person giving the critique is right, then you can work to improve yourself. If, however, you decide the criticism is unfounded, you have a few choices. Either you think the critic is incorrect, in which case you may decide to chalk the situation up to a difference of opinions and move on. If, on the other hand, you decide the critic is deliberately trying to be destructive in their criticism, then you can have a number of options. You can ignore them. After all, the problem is clearly theirs, and has nothing to do with you. Or you can challenge the criticism. If you feel you have to face your critic in order to stop them from being negative, then try to do so without emotion, use logic and explain why you feel you are being treated unfairly. Often, when faced with the irrefutable truth, people who criticise others unfairly will back down and realize they are in the wrong. Still, some people never learn and refuse to change even when they are in the wrong. In this case, all you can do is take their opinions with a grain of salt. The important thing is not to let their negative behavior change how you feel about yourself. This is probably easier said than done. If worse comes to worst you may have to minimise negative criticisers from your life where possible.

So far, we've talked about how to stop yourself from judging your flaws and how to ignore the criticism of those who aren't being constructive. Sometimes it isn't your shortcomings that make you feel bad about yourself. Sometimes it's the perfect lives and success of other people that makes you feel like a failure.

Why is it that seeing pictures of our old high school friends looking young and successful drives us crazy? Why do we secretly feel annoyed at hearing that the people we grew up with have become rich, remained youthful and seem to have perfect lives? Is it that, deep down, all we want is for them to fail? No. It's because we can't help comparing ourselves with our peers. It's okay for our friends to be happy and successful just as long as they aren't *too* successful. Why is that? Because if our peers have done more with their lives than we have, we can't help feeling like a failure. The problem is that people don't often convey the truth about themselves on social media. That picture of your high school nemesis looking like a supermodel in a bikini probably took twenty or more shots to achieve. Your old high school friends aren't likely to post about their failures on social media. You probably won't hear about the job promotion they were looked over for or the fact that they aren't coping as a parent. Social media is so skewed toward the positive that what people post is more fiction than reality.

The world of celebrity is even further removed from reality. Not only do models, actresses and influencers portray themselves in the best possible light, with full make up and optimal lighting, their images are airbrushed to the point where they no longer resemble the person being photographed. In fact, some airbrushing goes to such extremes that the resulting image isn't even anatomically possible. For instance, a Ralph Lauren ad featured a model whose hips were so airbrushed that they appeared to be smaller than her head.[2] These images are all around us, in magazines and advertisements all over the internet. The ideal image of beauty and masculinity are drummed into us constantly. Even if it's just on a subconscious level, we cannot help comparing ourselves to these images. It is clear that airbrushing and the high standard of beauty perpetuated by the fashion industry and media are responsible for creating body image problems. In fact, there has been an increase in hospital admission for anorexia nervosa by 33% in the last decade.[3] It's likely that the pressure to remain thin as perpetuated by social media has pushed people to go to extremes in order to meet an impossible standard. When you see a picture of a supermodel, or a celebrity, or even someone you know looking impossibly perfect, remember a single picture doesn't represent reality. No one is as perfect as their social media platform makes them seem. If you compare yourself to a celebrity, or even a friend or acquaintance on social media, you are being incredibly unfair to yourself. You are comparing yourself to something that isn't real. No one looks perfect 100% of the time. Not every mother is surrounded by smiling, happy, well-behaved children the way they appear on social media.

---

[2] "Ralph Lauren Apologizes For Image Of Emaciated Model: "We Are Responsible" (UPDATE)," *HuffPost*, March 18, 2010, https://www.huffpost.com/entry/emboing-boingem-and-ralph_n_311593.

[3] "Why is anorexia on the rise?" *Patient*, September 21, 2017, https://patient.info/news-and-features/why-is-anorexia-on-the-rise.

TIPS TO HELP YOU STOP COMPARING YOURSELF TO OTHERS

1. **Put Yourself First.** If you spend all of your time worrying about how you compare to others, you have less time to improve your own life. If you wanted to plant and grow a successful vegetable garden, you wouldn't spend all of your time staring at your neighbor's garden. Instead, you would clear the weeds, plant seeds and water your own garden. In the same way you shouldn't concentrate on how much someone else's life is better than yours. Instead, spend time, energy and effort improving your life. After all—you're worth it!

2. **Cut Back on Social Media.** If seeing friends, acquaintances and famous people on social media makes you feel inadequate, limit your time on it. Our biggest mistake with social media is that we tend to compare our everyday lives with other peoples' best moments. When viewing social media, try to be mindful of how the images you see trigger your inadequacy. If you feel yourself starting to feel down when comparing yourself, remind yourself that what you are seeing is a perfect moment in time, not someone's entire life.

3. **Be Thankful for the Good Things.** Human beings are always striving for more. Once our basic needs are met, humans constantly seek betterment. It's one of the reasons we're so successful. But this desire to do better can be our downfall, for it blinds us to everything we already have. Try to take a long, appreciative look at your life. Be glad for the friends and family you have. Be thankful that you have a roof over your

head and food to eat each day. Be glad that you have hopes and dreams and the chance to make your life even better.

4. **Don't Think You've Done Everything You Can.** You may not like the way your life is heading at the moment, but that doesn't mean you are stuck in a rut. There's always a chance to make a change for the better.

5. **Embrace the Past.** Sometimes the past can cloud our perception of the present. The mistakes we made in the past can haunt us. But our mistakes don't define us. The things we did, or the things that happened to us aren't who we are. They can make us grow. Be glad of your past. If you struggled or made mistakes, learn from them. Let them make you stronger. Appreciate how far you've come and look forward to how much further you are going to go!

6. **Use Comparison to Your Advantage.** If you look at someone and wish you could achieve the things that they have, don't let it get you down. Get inspired instead. If someone followed their dream, they probably put in a lot of time and effort to get where they are. You can do the same thing! Figure out what you want in life and go for it.

CHAPTER SUMMARY

In this chapter, you learned...

- To avoid feeling like a failure, stop comparing yourself to others
- Accepting your flaws will help you to move forward with positivity
- What you see on social media is fake, so there's no reason to be jealous

In the next chapter, you will learn...

- How to be proud of your achievements
- How to recognize your own success
- How to appreciate what you have

CHAPTER FOUR

BE PROUD OF YOUR ACHIEVEMENTS

If your friend told you he isn't good at anything and hasn't achieved anything with his life, what would you say to him? You'd probably reassure him and reel off a list of all the things he's done that are amazing. Being kind to others when they feel like a failure comes easy to us. But why can't we be as kind to ourselves? We're hard on ourselves because we've been trained to be modest. We're never happy with what we've achieved because society tells us we must always strive for more. We're much quicker to list our faults than we are to talk about our successes. But in order to be happy and healthy, we need to acknowledge our success.

If you've spent your life ignoring your achievements, it can be difficult to know where to begin to celebrate them. Try making a list of achievements you've made so far. Here is an example of an achievement list:

1. I passed my high school diploma.
2. I saved money and bought my first car.
3. I'm saving a deposit for a house.

4. I've given birth to twins and I'm a good mom.
5. I've started a new job.
6. I joined the gym and increased my strength and fitness.

Try to come up with a list of your own achievements.

Does it surprise you to see how much you've achieved? You're probably more successful than you thought. How does it make you feel to see all of your achievements? Pretty good? You should feel good.

It's not just the big things that you've done well. Every day your life is filled with achievements and success. Do you find that hard to believe? Well, it's true. We face challenges every day, we struggle, and most of the time we succeed. You may not think you have achieved much with your life, but you'd be surprised by how successful you are every day. In order for you to feel good about yourself and your achievements, it's important to change your way of thinking.

One way of seeing how successful you are is to write an achievement diary. Use your achievement diary to measure anything that you did which made you feel good about yourself or which made you feel proud. It doesn't have to be something major. It can be something small. For instance, if you manage to help your friend with a difficult personal problem that's an achievement. Or if you were able to turn an angry customer into a happy one, that's a great achievement. As you can see, not all achievements involve gaining wealth or prestige. Sometimes accomplishments are to do with helping people, overcoming obstacles or doing something to make your life better or easier.

You may be surprised how many achievements and small victories you have in a day. By noting them down in a diary you will realize just how successful you are. Below is an example of how you might fill out an achievement diary.

Day	Achievement 1	Achievement 2	Achievement 3	Achievement 4
Monday	I made my sales quota for the day at work.	I helped organize a bake sale for my son's high school.	I toilet trained my daughter.	At my weigh-in, I lost two pounds this week.
Tuesday	I mowed my elderly neighbor's lawn.	We made it out of the house on time this morning.		

As you look at the examples of the achievement diary, do you wonder if these are really achievements? Think about each one for a moment. Toilet training a toddler is no easy feat. It takes patience, calmness and the ability to reason. It takes time. It's frustrating. There are outside pressures. Everyone has an opinion on when your child should be out of nappies. The fact that you've successfully negotiated other people's (sometimes judgemental) opinions and managed to help your young child achieve a significant milestone is nothing to scoff at.

Take a look at another example. You might think mowing your neighbor's lawn isn't that big of a deal. And yet in this day and age we're all too busy. If you have a full-time job or a family, you don't have a lot of spare time. So, choosing to use up some of your own time to help out a neighbor is a really big achievement. You can also think about what it meant to the other person; in this example, I'm sure your neighbor was utterly delighted since it's a job they weren't able to do and now they can look out on a lovely mown lawn.

When you fill out your own achievement diary, think about what you've done each day that made you feel good about yourself. It doesn't matter how small the achievement is, write it in the diary.

When you look at things differently and adopt a more positive mindset, you can see how your days are filled with lots of achievements and wins. Once you start to recognize everyday success, you should begin to feel better about your life in general. You may still find it difficult to look at your life and judge how successful you are. Don't worry. We'll show you just how awesome you are with the following tips.

TIPS TO HELP YOU RECOGNIZE YOUR OWN SUCCESS

1. If you have difficulty acknowledging your own achievements, try viewing them as if someone else had accomplished them. We tend to be more generous about the achievements of others. Try to picture a friend of yours and think of how you'd view some of your accomplishments as if they were achieved by your friend.

2. One way to know that something is an achievement is to consider accolades. Have you achieved any awards or

acknowledgement for your work? Awards could include certificates, recognition (e.g. years of service) or achieving goals (e.g. sales numbers).

3. Improving the way something is done is a significant achievement. If you've thought up a new way of doing something at work, or at home, or with a hobby or sport you enjoy, this is a sign you've succeeded. For instance, if you've found a way to get a job done more efficiently it will save time in the workplace, allowing for more work to be done.

4. When your actions profit or improve life for others, this is another sign you've been successful. When you make a customer happy that means they are more likely to return and will also spread the word about the company you work for. The company you work for will prosper as a direct result of your actions!

5. Have you ever gone the extra mile, or taken on extra work? In your workplace, did you put up your hand and offer to do extra work in order to make things easier for others? Did someone ask you to do something extra, in addition to your ordinary work. It may seem like they're just giving you more to do, but being given extra responsibility in the workplace is a sign that you're trusted, valued and important. Or if you're a parent, did you volunteer to go on a field trip or contribute to a bake sale? Once more, your actions have made life better for others.

6. Have you overcome any obstacles or challenges in life? This is a major achievement. Being able to face adversity or hardship and come through it is one of the hardest things to do. Even if you feel at fault for the adversity, such as being addicted to drugs or alcohol, overcoming this obstacle is one of the hardest things to achieve in life. Life hands us all kinds of hurdles from injuries and accidents to unforeseen bad luck, sometimes our success is hindered by circumstances beyond our control. If the bumpy parts in the road of our journey slows down our achievements, it doesn't mean we've failed. Merely making it through these bumps is in itself an achievement.

As you become aware of your achievements, it's important to take the time to appreciate them. There are many ways to celebrate your achievements, including taking time for yourself. Treat yourself to a nice lunch, coffee or dinner. Include the friends or work-mates who've helped you achieve what you have. Or take the day off, just for yourself. Most of all, when you've achieved something in life you're proud of, allow yourself to *feel* it. Let the feeling of worthiness sweep over you and hold onto that feeling. Feel proud of yourself. Though it seems self-indulgent to celebrate your wins, there are many good reasons to give yourself a pat on the back when you've done well. Acknowledging your achievements gives you zeal—it fires you up to keep achieving. The more you acknowledge your success, the more you feel a duty to succeed. Celebrating achievements also makes you bolder; you will feel more confidence in your abilities and take more chances to succeed. The more you allow yourself to feel good about the things you do well, the more confidence, excitement, and drive you will have to keep doing well in life.

Part of feeling good about what you've achieved is being aware of the good things in your life. Humans are so successful because we strive for more. We never take the time to appreciate what we already have. We want bigger houses, nicer cars, and the latest high-end fashions. The entire economic system is hinged on feeding this need deep within us for *more*. This hunger for more is so strong that as soon as we achieve what we've longed for, we're already pondering what it is that we want next. In order to be happy, we need to appreciate what we already have. Instead of being happy with our lives, we tend to worry and fret over what we don't have. We wish our house was bigger, or that our vehicle was newer, or that we could have more money to live exactly how we want. The trouble with this is that we won't ever be happy with what we are about to get, unless we learn to be happy with what we already have.

So, if you feel like you don't have much, how do you learn to be happy with what you have? The best way is to change the way you think about what you already have. You need to learn to appreciate the benefits that are already in your life. If you have a home, this is a reason to be happy. If you have a job, you should feel lucky. It's a blessing to have a child or children, a gift to have a husband or wife, a joy to have a pet. Your health, if you can walk, run and move freely, is a reason to be grateful. If someone or something brings you joy or makes you laugh every day, you are fortunate indeed. Take the time to look around you, are you surrounded by people who make you happy, are there things around you that bring you comfort, warmth and joy.

41

You have a lot after all. You have so much to be grateful for—you deserve to enjoy it!

A good way to help you appreciate what you already have is to make some time to enjoy your surroundings. Turn off your devices and put social media aside. Take yourself to a comfortable place where you live, a nice warm spot in your garden, or a cozy corner of your favorite room. Sit and breathe in the air and smell the scent of your garden, or snuggle up in a warm blanket and allow yourself to enjoy the place and time where you are. Enjoy the small pleasures—the warble of a flock of birds will sound just as sweet in the garden of a mansion as it does in a more humble home.

CHAPTER SUMMARY

In this chapter, you learned...

- Listing your victories will help you be proud of what you've achieved
- Tips to help you recognize your success include picturing your success as someone else's
- Ways to appreciate what you have including feeling lucky that you have a job, friends and a home

In the next chapter, you will learn...

- How to accept failure
- How to approach the guilt of failing
- What's good about failing

CHAPTER FIVE

DON'T BEAT YOURSELF UP ABOUT FAILURE, LEARN FROM IT

No one succeeds at everything all the time. We all fail sometimes. You will fail sometimes. And that's okay. In fact, success often comes by way of failure. Scientists know this more than anyone. If scientists or inventors gave up as soon as an experiment failed, there wouldn't be any discoveries. We wouldn't have telephones, vehicles, airplanes, or any of the modern conveniences we take for granted. If scientists and inventors don't fret about failure, neither should you. Some of the most successful people have been failures. Many rich business people have been bankrupt in the past, which is about as big a failure as it gets financially speaking. Whatever you have failed at, even if you yourself have become bankrupt, there's always a way for you to rise up and become a success.

Of course, it's all very well to say failure isn't a bad thing. It's not so easy to accept failure as we've been raised in a society that punishes failure. If we don't meet a certain level in subjects at school we are given bad grades. This continues through to university where bad grades can mean failing and not graduating. In the workplace not meeting certain targets can mean losing wages and can even lead to termination. Since the consequences for failing are often negative, it's difficult to accept failure. But in order to move on from failure, that's exactly what we need to do; we need to accept it.

Accepting failure means to acknowledge the failure. It's okay to be annoyed that you've put time and effort into something that hasn't worked out the way you wanted. It's normal to be sad or heartbroken when your plans did not come to fruition, especially if you have not achieved something that you set your heart on. The important thing is not to let these feelings get the better of you. Acknowledge the fact that you may be sad, angry, frustrated and even confused and then let the feeling go. Don't dwell on it. Don't revisit it in an emotional way. Most of all, try to separate what happened with how you feel about yourself. You failed at something, but you are *not* a failure. A single incident, or even many incidents, do not have to define you.

Letting failure go is not the same as forgetting. In order to benefit from your failures, it's good to learn from them. If we don't learn from our failures, we will continue to make the same mistakes. Try to consider what happened from a place of logic, not emotion, separate from yourself.

HOW TO LEARN FROM FAILURE

- **Look at failure as a stepping stone toward success.** Sometimes in reaching our goals we take a few steps forward, only to be forced to take a step back. Sometimes we end up taking several steps back. As long as we have our goal in mind, however, we are still on the road to success.

- **Figure out what you can learn from your failure.** Were there things you could have done differently? Try to figure out where things went wrong. Can you think of more than one plan of action for the future? Maybe you did a few things wrong. It doesn't matter. As long as you realize your mistake, you're unlikely to repeat it.

- **Failing once can mean you're afraid to take risks in the future.** Don't let fear stop you from going after your dreams. Know you may get rejected or you may get things wrong. But not getting things right the first time is better than not trying at all. If you feel afraid of failing, try to do something with a small risk of failure and congratulate yourself on your achievements, no matter how small. For instance, try to cook a meal for your friends or family. There may be a small chance of failure but it won't matter because your friends and family will understand.

- **Use your failure to plan for future success.** What you've learned should help you figure out what to do next. You know what not to do, but you should also have a few clues about how to improve.

- **Change your thinking about failure.** Failure is a short-term hold up. If you have a goal in mind, then everything you do along the way is just a step on the road to success. Failure can be positive. It can make you more motivated to succeed. It can help you come up with an even better strategy than if you hadn't failed. There are plenty of examples of people who have failed and gone on to create something new that bought them equal if not more success. When Steve Jobs, the creator of the incomparably successful Apple company, was fired as the CEO of the company he started, he didn't give up and hang his head in shame. Instead, he moved on and founded NeXt and Pixar. In the end, he even became the CEO of Apple once more. His failure didn't end his career; it motivated him to achieve even more. Abraham Lincoln's failures were many, as well. He failed in business, had a nervous breakdown, and was defeated in his run for president. Yet, it's arguable he went on to become one of the most celebrated American presidents of all time. Like Jobs and Lincoln, you too can use your low points as motivation to do better than you ever imagined.

- **Reassess what you want.** You may find that not achieving something can change your perspective of what's important. It isn't until you try something that you realize it may not be for you. Some jobs aren't what you imagine them to be. Maybe you haven't achieved your best because the career you chose isn't the one you're meant for. For instance, perhaps you always dreamed of being a lawyer only to find that once you begin practicing law that you aren't successful. It might be that you aren't cutthroat enough. Instead of being upset about failing as a lawyer, you could try to figure out what it is you're really good at. You could try a career that is about helping people or a career in the arts. Sometimes failure can make us change direction completely and lead us to try something we never would have thought of otherwise.

- **Failure helps give you a reality check.** When we don't succeed at something, it tells us we may need to try a different approach or even put in more effort. Failing at an exam in school tells us we may need to put in more hours of study or that we might need help from a tutor or loved one. Not succeeding at something may also shed light on our true desires. If you thought you wanted to go to university and you failed your entrance exams, it doesn't mean you're a failure. It might mean you don't really want to go to university, or perhaps university isn't really the right thing for you. A good way to know if what you've failed at is not actually something you want is to reflect on how you really feel about not achieving it. If you feel relief, apathy or even happiness, there's a good chance you never really wanted the thing you were aiming for after all! Failure can also help to steer us toward the things we are better at, as well as the things we enjoy more and that come naturally to us.

- **Not winning or achieving is character building.** It can make you stronger. Being challenged by a lack of achievement is a test. It will test your resolve, your courage and your resilience. It can make you better at becoming more tenacious and continuing to fight for what you want. If you learn to fail and hold your head up high, you'll be less likely to fear things in the future. You'll be brave and you may take risks. After all, you've learned that not winning isn't the worst thing in the world.

- **Failure makes us feel even better about our successes.** One of the biggest positives of failure is that it can make you grateful when you do eventually achieve what you want. If you keep failing, but don't give up, learn from your mistakes and come up with new strategies and eventually you should succeed. And when you do succeed after so much trial and effort, your achievement will be all the sweeter.

DON'T LET FAILURE MAKE YOU FEEL GUILTY

Guilt is a powerful emotion. When we fail at something, we often feel like we've let other people or ourselves down. Failure is a part of life, mistakes happen, errors and mishaps lead to learning. We should never feel guilty for something that is a normal part of life.

What is it that makes us feel guilty about failure? Usually it has to do with how other people see us. We are most wracked with guilt when we think of how others might perceive our failure. There are occasions when our guilt over failure might be more likely to arise. Events or occasions where we have to meet with people we haven't seen for a while might spark feelings of guilt over failure. Events like weddings, reunions or even just social occasions like lunches can all bring our lack of success to the forefront. When people haven't seen each other for a while it's natural for them to ask each other how things are going. Just a simple question like, "How have you been?" can spark feelings of inadequacy and guilt if we feel we haven't accomplished something we should.

How should we negotiate situations that might highlight our failures and make us feel bad? For instance, if someone asks how your job was going when you were just fired, it can be a difficult question to answer. You will naturally feel ashamed and then reluctant to explain your situation. Even though there may be a good reason for losing your job—perhaps the company, through no fault of yours, failed and could no longer employ you—you still feel embarrassed having to explain this to other people. The best thing in this situation is to remind yourself that your job doesn't define you. You weren't to blame for being fired. You can say something simple, like there wasn't enough work to keep you employed and that you're excited for the future. This may not entirely be true, but it might be eventually. There's every chance you'll get another job. There's every chance you'll do well in the future. So, there's no reason to feel guilty or bad about what others think of your failure.

CHAPTER SUMMARY

In this chapter, you learned…

- Accept failure by acknowledging it, working through your emotions, and then letting it go
- Let go of guilt over failing
- Know that failure is a stepping stone to success

In the next chapter, you will learn…

- How to look forward, not back
- How to forgive others
- How to forgive yourself
- How to take action for a better future

CHAPTER SIX

LOOK FORWARD, NOT BACK

Once you've accepted the past and embraced the hardships that have made you who you are today, let the past go. Yes, the past has shaped you and made you who you are. Yes, some of that may feel like it's held you back or made you achieve less in life, but it's best not to let the negative things that have happened define us. If something happened in the past that stopped you from being as successful as you'd like to be, that is in the past. Now it's time to move on. Take your first steps toward the future. Don't let your forward momentum be bogged down by the past. Take a big, bold step into your best life.

It sounds simple, but one of the best ways to stop dwelling on the past is to focus on the future. If you find yourself getting bogged down on things that happened in the past, turn your thoughts to the good things that are to come. Is there something you're looking forward to in the near future? Do you have plans to go on holiday or to take a day trip somewhere nice? If you feel you don't have anything specific to look forward to in the near future, why not make plans? Is there something you've been wanting to do for a while, plans you've been putting off because you're too busy? Why not set yourself a future goal, something really special that you can focus on? It's hard not to dwell on the past if you don't have anything drawing you toward the future. Once you learn to start living life for smaller pleasures, you can move on to making some bigger goals.

The present is a good place to turn your attention away from the past. Before going forward, you need to learn to be happy with where you are. If you think too much about how your past has affected your present in a negative way, you may find yourself caught in an endless cycle. The future can be whatever you want it to be, but if you can't be happy right now, it'll be hard to build a positive future. Living in the moment with positivity will help you feel happy in the now. If you start the day on a positive note and concentrate on the good things with intention, you will start to see the present in a positive light.

One of the things that can keep us stuck in the past is fixation on how others have wronged us. We may blame others for where we are in life. We may blame others for ruining our lives or getting in the way of opportunities we might have taken. In order to move on, there's only one thing we can do: we must forgive. Forgiveness will help you live in the present. If you forgive people from the past, the past can no longer have a hold on you. It may be difficult. Someone may have done you wrong in a significant way, they may have hurt you so badly you'd think it impossible to forgive. But forgiving people, even under the worst circumstances, will not only free you from the power of any negativity associated with the past, it will give you power over that past, as well. If someone harmed you, that is their fault. But if you let that past continue to haunt and pain you every day, that is on you.

In fact, forgiving someone isn't only good for helping you to look toward the future with positivity. Learning to forgive others can even have a big impact on our health. Studies have shown that forgiving others who you have perceived to have wronged you may improve many areas of your health, including anxiety, stress, negative emotions and, interestingly, cardiovascular problems and immune system function. What this means is that hanging on to grudges against others is harmful to our health as well as our minds. When we don't forgive people, our heart and cardiovascular systems are at risk. So, not only is forgiveness a good idea if you want to move on with your life, it's crucial to your physical health and mental wellbeing. These studies also showed that when people were experiencing the emotions that go with unforgiveness, their arterial blood pressure was higher. This means that when we hold onto grudges and give in to feelings of unforgiveness we are actually making ourselves less healthy. The best thing in order for you to move on to a happy and healthy future is to forgive.

TIPS FOR HOW TO FORGIVE OTHERS TO IMPROVE YOUR HEALTH AND HAPPINESS

1. **Let go of your negative emotions.** Forgiveness is about showing clemency to another, even if they don't deserve it. Forgiveness doesn't mean you have to forget what happened. Nor does it mean you should think the pain they caused means nothing. What it means is letting go of anger, grief and desire for revenge. Such emotions tend to eat away at us and do us harm.

2. **Show empathy.** One way to help forgive someone is to learn to empathize with them. If you can try to figure out what has happened to someone in their life, and if you can understand and feel what they have gone through, then you are likely to be able to forgive them. If they have had a difficult life, it has affected them negatively and caused them to do harm to you.

3. **Learn from the past.** Sometimes when people hurt us, we need to learn from the experience to avoid the same thing from happening again. We can put boundaries in place with those who have hurt us in order to avoid future hurt. Boundaries will allow us to continue to have a relationship with someone in the future. For instance, if someone hurt you by stealing from you, you may decide not to allow them into your house in future. Instead you may make it a rule to meet somewhere neutral.

4. **Be patient.** Forgiveness is a process that takes time and is an emotional skill that needs to be learned. When you decide to forgive those who hurt you, it may pay to try learning how to forgive someone who has not hurt you too gravely.

5. **Accept what happened.** In order to forgive, you must accept what happened to you. Accepting it means to acknowledge what happened to you without getting emotional or angry and without denying it or trying to push down the hurt. Use empathy to walk in the shoes of the person who wronged you. Try to imagine what they were thinking and why, in a non-judgemental way, when they hurt you. Now, try to let it go.

You may want to speak the words of forgiveness aloud by mentioning by name the one who wronged you and declaring forgiveness. Feel the weight of pain and anguish release as you speak these words and let a feeling of lightness and freedom wash over you.

6. **Show compassion.** Once you have let the pain of being hurt go, the next step is to learn to feel compassion for the one who has hurt you. Depending on how much they have harmed you, this may be incredibly difficult. Try to understand that the hurt they have caused is harming them. Consider that it has probably come from a place of pain and suffering. Compassion will allow you to take yourself out of the equation. You should try to see the person who hurt you as separate and not to take personally what they did. The pain they caused is their issue, their problem, and not your fault.

7. **Express goodwill.** Some people find sending love, light, or positive vibes to those who have harmed them is a good final step in ultimately forgiving someone. Wishing love on those who have hurt you is the ultimate way to love yourself. It's difficult, but when you have reached this point, the point of truly wishing well to the ones who have harmed you, you are ready to be completely free.

LEARN TO LET GO OF YOUR MISTAKES

It isn't just those who have wronged us that we should forgive. We must also learn how to forgive ourselves. There are a number of stages to go through in forgiving yourself. Sometimes forgiving ourselves is the hardest thing of all. But you deserve to give yourself a break. Try these tips to help you let go of your mistakes.

1. **Speak your mistake out loud.** Speaking out loud the things we'd rather forget makes us face up to them in a concrete way we can't avoid. You may find yourself feeling emotional as you say out loud what you've been avoiding acknowledging. These emotions are good and are all part of the healing process. Don't fight them, go with them.

2. **Start small.** If you find forgiving yourself for a particular mistake is too difficult, try to work on less emotionally upsetting mistakes. Place the thing you can't quite face right now in a metaphorical box, close the lid, and let it wait until you are ready to acknowledge it. This way you can practice forgiving yourself.

3. **Be kind to yourself.** You may feel like something you have done makes you a bad person. If you feel upset about your mistakes it's a clear sign you have empathy and care for others, which makes you a good person, one who is worthy of forgiveness.

4. **Talk to your negative inner voice.** Treat your negative voice like someone who's hurting you, because you really are damaging yourself by being critical. This is a way of giving empathy to yourself and will help you identify the triggers for negative self-talk.

Learning to enjoy your present life will help you let go of the past and thrive in the moment. If you don't enjoy your job, see if you can find another one or find a way to make your current job better. If you don't like where you live, try to improve your conditions by either making them better or working toward moving somewhere better. If your relationships are not enjoyable, try to work on them.

HOW TO TAKE ACTION NOW FOR A BETTER FUTURE

The past can bog us down. We make assumptions about ourselves based on what we perceive to be our failures and mistakes. Yet, oftentimes circumstances are as much to blame for the way things go wrong as we are. For instance, we may not succeed in a business venture for a number of reasons. The political and economic climate can affect how well a product sells. There may be factors beyond our control which made success highly unlikely regardless of anything we were able to do. Even when we know the cause may not be our fault it can still be difficult to get over failure. There are many outcomes to failure such as financial—a lot of money can be lost in a failed venture. We can end up doubting ourselves when we fail and think we simply aren't made to succeed in many areas of our lives. Failure feels bad. Once we've failed, we probably want to avoid the feeling in the future. Fear of failure can hold us back from achieving our goals.

How do we overcome our fear of failure in order to succeed and take control of our lives? Firstly, you must learn to take risks again. In order to do this, you need to re-evaluate how you see failure. If you see failure as linked to your prestige, then you will take any lack of success personally. If you see failure as inevitable, you won't be able to try anything new or risky. Thinking you are bound to fail can be a self-fulfilling prophecy. If you think you are hopeless, then you will lack the confidence and positivity needed to succeed. Try not to let past failures dictate your future.

Begin undoing your fear of failure by taking small risks. If you feel like a social failure due to the loss of an important friendship, take a small step in making new friends. Try a new hobby that will bring you in contact with people, enabling you to socialize without too much pressure. If you're afraid of failing in a weight loss goal, try to take smaller steps in changing your lifestyle and be happy with any success you have, no matter how small. If you've been out of the workforce for a long time, instead of taking on full time work, start off with a part time job.

The next step is to start to make new memories to replace the old, less successful ones. Rewrite how you see yourself by becoming the success you feared you would never be. The more you succeed every day, even in a small way, the more you will see yourself as a success. Help to ensure this success by making sure your goals are achievable. Start with small, easy goals. Try to make a list of small goals you can achieve, there are some examples below to help you get started.

1. I want to make sure I get to bed early each night so I get enough sleep.
2. I want to be more organized in the morning by preparing the night before.
3. I want to go for a run at least three times a week.
4. I want to join a volunteer organization and meet new people.

5. I want to go to night school and study in order to find a better job.

6. I want to cut down on how many cigarettes I have each day so I can eventually quit altogether.

7. I want to eat more vegetables and get healthy.

CHAPTER SUMMARY

In this chapter, you learned…

- Look forward by focussing on the future instead of the past
- Forgive people by letting go of your anger so the past can't have a hold on you
- Forgive yourself by speaking your mistakes out loud and letting them go
- Overcome fear of failure by taking small risks and building up to greater success

In the next chapter, you will learn…

- The benefits of taking "time off"
- Why you deserve "me time"
- How to enjoy "me time"

CHAPTER SEVEN

DON'T FEEL GUILTY ABOUT TAKING TIME OFF

We lead busy lives. We're expected to put in long hours at work while raising a family. The drive to succeed in making money and advancing our careers while being the perfect parent, partner, maintaining a household, doing chores and errands leaves us little time for ourselves. With a high demand on our time and so much to do each day, it can feel like we're letting the side down if we take too much time for ourselves. If we try to take even an hour out of our day to recharge we may always have the niggling feeling that there's something else we should be doing. This can cause stress and guilt, making us think of ourselves as failures for letting work and other responsibilities fall behind.

So, what happens if we take time off when we have a lot to do? We tend to feel tense. We don't relax and allow ourselves to enjoy our time off. This means we can end up feeling even less refreshed and happy than if we hadn't tried to relax in the first place! So, what's the solution? All too often when guilt stops us from relaxing, we give in to the pressure and plough on with the chores and tasks we're meant to be doing. After all, what is the point in taking time off if we can't even enjoy it?

We need to learn how to take time for ourselves. We need to learn how to have a good time again. The first step in learning how to take time off is letting go of the guilt. The best way to do this is to consider the fact that not only is taking time to recharge our batteries good for us, it may make us better at the things we should be doing. It also makes us more relaxed and productive.

THE BENEFITS OF TAKING TIME OFF

Taking time out will allow you to strengthen your relationship with loved ones. Your partner, children, friends and family will benefit from spending quality time with you. This will have a positive effect on their lives as well as yours. Close relationships require work and effort. If you spend family time in a rush, trying to move on to the next work or other task, you won't be forging a strong bond with those you love. If you put aside some time to be with your loved ones they will be much happier and you will have a closer relationship.

If we don't take time off, we run the risk of burning out. When the work is piled up, we tend to push through, trying to get as much done as we can. But eventually, if we don't slow down and recharge, our productivity goes down, we make more mistakes and we can't think as clearly or work as well. In one study, long work hours result in less productivity. Working for more than fifty hours a week causes an abrupt drop off in productivity, and doing more than fifty-five hours work a week results in so little productivity that it's not even worth doing. Even when you work a "normal" forty-hour week, if you have lots of other responsibilities, like childcare and housework, you can end up just as burned out.

Having time off will make you more inclined to work more effectively or imaginatively. Google is known for allowing its employees to take time off to pursue their own interests. As a result, when they are at work they can function better; they can think outside of the box and in a more effective way. If it's okay for the employees of one of the most successful companies in the world to take time out for fun and relaxation it should be okay for you!

Taking time out for yourself will allow your brain to function better. If you overdo it at work, you'll find everyday tasks take longer, and you'll make more mistakes. In other areas of your life that are high demand and stressful, such as parenting, you'll find you can't cope so well if you don't take time for yourself. For instance, you will be less able to cope with a child's tantrums if you don't give yourself the chance to unwind.

Without "me time," all you have is stress and mundanity. If your life is fast-paced and highly demanding, then your stress levels may go through the roof. Without giving yourself the opportunity to unwind, you may end up causing yourself physical harm. Stress has mental and physical consequences. For instance, if we are in a constant state of stress, we can experience physical symptoms like heart palpitations, frequent infections and illness, digestive and stomach problems like irritable bowel syndrome, panic attacks, high blood-pressure, stomach ulcers and mental health problems like depression and anxiety.

Increased happiness makes us kinder and better at relating to others. We have more empathy with others if we are fulfilled and content in our lives. If we don't get the chance to enjoy life, there's little opportunity for happiness. By simply making time for ourselves, we make ourselves better people. This will improve our working lives and private lives.

Taking time off means you can discover new things about yourself. If you start a hobby, you might find you're especially good at something you would've never tried before. You may get to meet new people and go to new places which will broaden your horizons. You never know where life can take you if you allow yourself to be adventurous and to try new things purely for fun.

If we don't allow ourselves to find joy in life, we can become unenthusiastic about everyday life because we don't have much to look forward to. If we don't allow ourselves to enjoy life, we can feel like we're just going through the motions. We start to feel hollow or empty, and this can filter down into our working and personal lives. On the other hand, if we allow fun and enjoyment into our lives, without guilt or the feeling that we're doing something we shouldn't be doing, then there are many physical and mental benefits. Allowing yourself to enjoy "me time" will nurture your soul. It will make you more relaxed, happy and fulfilled.

YOU DESERVE TO ENJOY ME TIME

The idea that you do not deserve "me time" may be something you struggle with. The idea that we need to meet all of our goals in order to be rewarded can prevent us from allowing ourselves to unwind. We think we have to excel in every area of our lives in order to feel like we've achieved anything. A tendency toward perfectionism can make it difficult for us to recognize when we've done well. If we never acknowledge our own worth, then we won't ever feel worthy of being rewarded with "me time" or any other form of self-care. The problem is we often have so much going on. Long hours at work, juggling family and other responsibilities makes it hard for us to be 100% good at everything all of the time. We need to learn to be happy that we're trying our best. The truth is, you're probably doing much better than you think. If you have a lot to do, cut yourself some slack.

If you find it difficult to believe you deserve "me time," consider a few of the reasons why you deserve to give yourself a break:

- If you work hard, regardless of what you think you've achieved, you have earned some time to relax and unwind.

- If you have helped others — neighbors, children, family, clients or colleagues — you have earned the right to have a breather, to put your feet up and let yourself breathe.

- If you volunteer, you've given your free time to make someone else's life better, so you deserve to indulge yourself. Give some time back to yourself, too.

- If you have struggled to get things done around the home including housework, cooking, doing washing, and other chores, you deserve to put your feet up!

- If you have kept smiling when things went wrong and you tried to stay positive during a difficult situation, you've probably made life easier for others. Reward your awesome attitude with a well-earned break.

WAYS TO ENJOY TIME FOR YOU

Sometimes, we feel like if we do have time off we have to do something momentous with it, but that's not always the case. If it makes you happy—do it. You don't have to travel to exotic places or do exciting, adrenaline filled things to get the most out of your time alone. Although if you find sky-diving relaxing, by all means, enjoy it! There are many other ways for you to recharge. Just remember, whatever you choose to do, as long as it makes you feel happy and relaxed, it's okay. If lying in a bath reading a good book makes you happy and recharges your batteries, go for it!

Here are a few ideas for activities you can do to unwind:

- Boost your creativity: knit, crochet, paint, draw or write poetry.

- Exercise for fun. Going for a swim, especially if it's in a river or the sea, is a great way to get the blood pumping, feel refreshed and have fun.

- Think happy, positive thoughts. Daydream about something you enjoy to do or relive a fond memory.

- Pamper yourself at home or at a spa. If visiting a spa is not affordable, or too difficult, give yourself your own spa day at home. Have a facial, deep condition your hair, use a massage machine, or better yet get a back rub from a loved one!

- Listen to music, dance with abandon and sing with joy or passionate emotion. Let go!

- Take a nap. If you lead a busy life, it's likely you're operating on less than optimal sleep. Taking a nap can refresh your brain, relax you and make you feel more energetic.

- Catch up with a friend. We rarely have time to just hang out with people once we're adults. But spending some time chatting, having coffee and kicking back is one of the best ways to feel more like your old self.

- Play a game. Board games aren't just for kids. They are a great way to entertain yourself with a bit of fun competition.

TIPS TO FIT IN TIME FOR YOURSELF

Hopefully, you're convinced you deserve some time to yourself. But if your life is hectic it may seem impossible to fit in some "me time."

In order to make time for yourself, it's important to prioritize. Look at your daily schedule and see if there's any way to save more time. For instance, you might consider cutting down your time on social media. Although browsing social media sites may be a form of taking time for yourself, it's all too easy to spend the hours in this way. Next, you might consider learning to delegate. If you're the only one who does housework in your family or among housemates, try to get those you live with to take on some of your tasks.

One of the most difficult things is learning to say "no." If you're one of those people who always says "yes," even when you know you have too much on your hands, try to force yourself to say "no" more often. You have to learn to prioritise "me time." Don't see it as something you can sacrifice in order to help someone else. Make sure you schedule your down time for a specific hour of the day and stick to that. If someone asks if you can help them, tell them you have an appointment; they don't need to know the appointment you have is with yourself!

If you're really rushed, take small breaks to fit in your "me time." If you have a lot on your hands with work, family and other commitments, it could be too much to try to fit in an hour at the spa. You could, however, try to grab yourself fifteen minutes to yourself here and there.

CHAPTER SUMMARY

In this chapter, you learned...

- Time out has many benefits, including preventing burnouts, avoiding mistakes and being able to get closer to family.
- "Me time" is necessary for many reasons. For example, you deserve a break for working hard.
- There are many ways to enjoy "me time." For instance, exercising for fun.

In the next chapter, you will learn...

- What self-worth really means
- How to gain self-worth
- That it's okay to have self-worth
- How to treat yourself well

71

CHAPTER EIGHT

GAIN SELF-WORTH BY REALIZING IT'S OKAY TO LOVE YOURSELF

People often mistakenly judge their own worth based on outside factors and actions rather than their inherent worth as a person. Self-worth is about *you*, not what you have or what you do. For instance, we should not judge our self-worth by the job we happen to be doing. Self-worth should not be determined by outside factors like your grades, your finances, your health, your accomplishments or your friendships. Failure can affect your feeling of self-worth. For instance, failing a driving test might make you feel worthless. Or money problems might make you feel like a financial failure. These feelings of failure may lower your opinion of yourself and damage how worthy you feel you are. But let's look at these examples a little more closely. What does failing a driving test say about you? Does it say you aren't a worthwhile person? No, it does not. Numerous outside factors can be blamed for failing a driving test. Being nervous about failing a test can affect the outcome. What about if you're so bad with money you end up in debt? Does that make you a less worthwhile person? Again, the answer is no. Having difficulty managing money does not make you less worthy. All it means is that you need a little education on how to manage money. Taking a budgeting course or money advice will soon fix the problem. So being bad with money isn't a character flaw, it's a learning experience.

Our own self-worth shouldn't be something that depends on other people. Too often people judge themselves against others in order to measure their own self-worth. The problem with this is that there will always be somebody who you perceive to be better-looking than you, funnier than you or more successful than you. Using comparison to gauge your own self-worth doesn't just lower your self-esteem, it can actually be harmful. According to a study carried out at the University of Michigan, students who judged their own self-worth against outside sources, like academic achievement and their appearance, described being under more stress, having anger issues and relationship problems as well as academic problems. They were also more likely to have problems with drug and alcohol abuse and eating disorders. Conversely, participants in the study who judged their self-worth internally (by looking inward) were happier, did better academically and were less likely to experience drug and alcohol problems. What this means is that we should not look to outside sources to find out what we're worth. We should judge ourselves based on just one factor: ourselves.

HOW TO GAIN SELF-WORTH

If we shouldn't judge ourselves by other people, how else can we figure out our self-worth? What we need to do is put in place something you learned in an earlier chapter. In order to judge your self-worth, you need to silence your inner critic. Stop listening to that voice in your head telling you that you aren't as good as other people. Instead, try to figure out what it is that's good about you—regardless of how you feel about other people. Don't ask yourself if you're as attractive as someone else. Don't ask yourself if you're as funny as someone else. Ask yourself, instead, what it is that you like about yourself. If you want to judge your appearance, think about what you like about yourself. Do you like the color of your eyes, or the dimple on your chin? Do you think you have a fun, dry sense of humor? Then feel good about this. Think about these things when you consider your self-worth and don't be tempted to compare these things with the same traits in other people.

Try to make a list of things you like about yourself. Don't question whether anyone else would agree with this list. Don't compare yourself when you think of your attributes. This is just about you. Here is an example of some of the things you might write about yourself that are positive:

1. I am good at writing.
2. I am good at poetry.
3. I am kind.
4. I am a good listener.
5. I am good with children.
6. I am funny.
7. I am good with numbers.
8. I pick up new things quickly.

Are you surprised by how many things you like about yourself? Does it make you feel any differently, seeing how much there is to love about you? You should feel good. There's nothing wrong with knowing what's great about you!

If you find it difficult to come up with something positive about yourself, it's not because there's nothing good about you. It just means you're being a little hard on yourself. Maybe you could try to ask someone close to you, who you trust, to tell you some of the good things about you. Now you really will find out how awesome you are!

YOU ARE WORTH IT

One of the main barriers to gaining self-worth is the idea that it's somehow self-absorbent to acknowledge the good things about yourself. You may not think you deserve to feel good about yourself. There are many reasons to feel like you don't deserve self-love. The way you have been treated by people in the past, the people from your childhood, your peers, family members and teachers, for instance, may all have made you feel less self-confident. You may not think it—but you are worthy of self-love.

The first stage in learning self-love and self-worth is not to fear it. Loving yourself does not mean you are selfish or narcissistic. Self-love isn't narcissistic because it isn't about showing off or preening. It's about giving yourself the same consideration, respect and care that you give to other people.

Having self-worth means you have to learn to trust yourself. Trust yourself to judge your own decisions instead of letting others tell you how you should think, feel, dress and act. If you learn to listen to yourself then you will be less likely to be taken advantage of or used by other people. You will also be more likely to stand by your own convictions and not allow yourself to be talked into things you don't want to do. Being able to listen to yourself and know your boundaries means you can communicate your limits to other people.

Building self-confidence will help you bolster your sense of self-worth. Learning to block negativity is the best way to keep your self-confidence from eroding. You've already learned about negative self-talk and how to block it. Now you must also try to block the negativity from others. This can be hard to do. When someone says things that demean you, or if they judge you negatively, it's hard not to take it personally. In this case, the issue is theirs, not yours. You may have to surround yourself with positivity. Surround yourself with people who are kind and make you feel good about yourself. Don't give too much energy or thought to those who are negative toward you. Try to banish the negative words and actions from other people from your mind. Though you must still stand up for yourself, that's part of knowing your self-worth, but you need not expend any more energy than you have to on people who aren't positive.

Gain self-confidence by setting goals you can achieve. If you achieve the things you set out to, this makes you feel good about yourself and will help push you toward achieving your other goals. Push yourself a little and you may be surprised how awesome you can be. Try a new hobby, meet new people.

Self-confidence comes from not just achieving your goals and feeling good about yourself. It also comes from being able to handle negativity. Building up your resilience to negative situations and negative people will prevent you from losing self-confidence. If you can be strong in the face of negativity and avoid letting negative people or situations get you down, your sense of self-worth will be stronger.

An excellent way to boost your own sense of self-worth is to treat yourself well. Give yourself an extra moment to smell the scent of flowers on a spring morning. If you don't treat yourself well, then you won't believe it when you try to convince yourself that you are worthy. Prove to yourself that you are worth it.

TIPS TO TREAT YOURSELF WELL

- **Consider your needs and how to meet them.** At work, in the home and in the community, we often put emphasis on helping others, whether others be friends, family or clients and customers. To prove to yourself that you are worthy of your own love, make time for yourself. Make sure your needs are met. Think about what you really want, and take steps to achieve your wants. Some wants and needs might be large ones, such as you might want to find a job that might better meet your need for social interaction. Other desires can be small, everyday things, like you might want to get more sleep, but you feel like pressures in your life mean you have to keep on going. Instead of putting everything else ahead of your health, make sure you set a bedtime and stick to it. Don't put yourself last. You deserve to be taken care of—by you.

- **Treat yourself like a friend.** You wouldn't ignore your friend's needs, so don't ignore your needs. You would want your friend to be comfortable, happy and relaxed. Try to consider your feelings just like you would a friend's. If your friend looked sad or stressed, you wouldn't ignore their emotions. You would try to cheer them up and help them get to the bottom of the problem. Be your own friend when you're feeling down or in need of help. Help yourself.

- **If you want to love yourself, let others show love to you.** We're programmed to be modest when it comes to compliments. Instead of denying a complement as soon as it's given, thank the person who paid you the compliment and accept it. We become so good at being modest that pretty soon we refuse to believe it when people say nice things to us. If you won't believe other people when they tell you you're great, you won't believe yourself. If you have trouble believing the nice things people say about you, try writing down the positive things people say about you. Read back over your book of compliments whenever you begin to doubt yourself.

- **Get to know you.** If you don't know yourself, it's hard to love yourself. Figure out your core values. What is it you care about? Where is your place in the world? What are your spiritual needs? If you have some higher purpose, it can help you feel like you are worthy, because you aren't just living day by day. You're contributing in a meaningful way. If you learn about your core, inner values, you will be stronger and more able to build healthy boundaries around other people. As soon as you know who you are, you will be able to let other people into your life in a healthy way.

- **Learn to love yourself.** We generally reserve unconditional love for close family members and loved ones. But you can love yourself unconditionally, too. Loving yourself unconditionally means you will love yourself no matter what. Don't withdraw positive feelings toward yourself based on the things you've done. Instead, face up to any mistakes, learn and move on without withdrawing the feeling of love you have toward yourself. We all make mistakes. If we feel bad, that's normal, but we don't need to beat ourselves up for too long. Letting your heart be full of love and compassion for yourself when you are at your worst is the best way to ensure you have a healthy sense of self-worth that will endure anything.

Having self-worth means you know you are a worthy human being, no matter what you look like, where you live or what you do.

CHAPTER SUMMARY

In this chapter, you learned…

- Self-worth isn't about what you have or what you do; it's about *you*.
- Gain self-worth by increasing your self-esteem.
- You deserve to have a sense of self-worth because you deserve to feel good about yourself.
- There are many ways to treat yourself well. For instance, try to treat yourself with the same consideration as you would a friend.

In the next chapter, you will learn…

- About the many positive effects of thinking positively
- How to think positively
- How to act more positively
- How to boost your positivity

CHAPTER NINE

THINK POSITIVE

When terrible things happen in the world around us, it might seem impossible to have a positive outlook on life. There are many things you can't control, but can control your mindset. You can choose to be negative, or you can choose to be positive. You've already learned about controlling your negative self-talk, which is a big step in the right direction toward positive thinking. The next step is to turn the way you speak and act, think and feel, into the opposite of negative self-talk.

THE EFFECTS OF THINKING POSITIVELY

Before we discuss how to turn your thoughts into positive ones, let's take a look at why thinking positively is so important.

1. **Improve your health.** There are many health benefits to be had from thinking in a positive way. Researchers found that people who are more positive are less inclined to suffer and die from serious illnesses, such as lung cancer, ovarian cancer, respiratory diseases, stroke, breast cancer, colorectal cancer,

infection and heart disease. The overall physical and mental health of those with a positive mindset was found to be better with lower rates of depression, and increased levels of immunity.

2. **Foster relationships.** Positive people tend to have better relationships with others. People are drawn to those who make them feel good. So being positive will make people want to be around you. You'll also find your positivity rubbing off on others—causing them to be more uplifting and improving their lives. Positive people also tend to attract people romantically and they have better relationships with improved communication.

3. **Overcome adversity.** You will be able to focus better if you have a positive frame of mind. Negativity tends to eat away at us. When we are negative, we tend to dwell on the bad things and worry over them instead of trying to come up with a solution and moving on. With positivity, you can handle the bad things more effectively with a clearer mind to find a solution.

4. **Increase productivity.** Positive people tend to be more successful in all areas of life. Thinking something will go well and being positive helps you get your job done and keeps you focussed. When you're positive, those around you are more inclined to want to help you and listen to your point of view.

5. **Improve your quality of life.** Optimistic people have a more peaceful and fulfilled life. You will be happier every day if you approach life thinking everything is going to go well. If you stay positive your day will run more smoothly, you will feel less tired and more energized.

6. **Achieve more.** Positive thinking focusses your behavior on the things you want in life. Negative thinking makes you worried about your current situation and pessimistic about the future. Negative thinkers may feel helpless as if there's little they can do to change their lot. Whereas optimists tend to look toward the good things they imagine they will achieve.

7. **Become more adventurous and open-minded.** When you are optimistic, you are more open to new ideas. You are more likely to want to broaden your horizons and improve your life. This openness will expose you to new ideas and experiences that will enrich and change your life. You may be more open to travel, friendships, learning new things and making big changes for the better. Despite being able to see that their lives aren't so positive, people who think negatively are less likely to act in order to change their lives. This is because negative people struggle to see a future that's positive. With a positive mindset, you can make your life everything you ever dreamed of!

As you can see, there are many good reasons for taking on a more positive mindset. Not everyone finds it easy to think positively. The way we've been raised, negative life experiences, and our own temperament all determine how optimistic we are. If you've been through a lot of hardship and pain in your life, it's understandable that you may not have such a cheery outlook on the future. But you can learn to see things more positively, no matter what you've been through or where you've come from in life.

HOW TO THINK MORE POSITIVELY

Living in the moment is a sure way to keep negative thoughts at bay. Being present will stop you from looking back at the negative aspects of the past. Living for the moment will also prevent you from thinking too much about the future. If you can learn to truly experience the present, you will be able to see the beauty and good in the world around you. Meditation, which we will talk more about in a later chapter, is a great way to teach you how to live for today. There are many excellent forms of mediation that will take you away from the past and future by teaching you how to concentrate on what is happening in the world around you right now.

In order to think positively, you need to practice thinking optimistically. In the same way that you must train your body, you also need to teach your mind how to think positively. Negative people tend to describe good things that happen to them as occurring from an outside source. Positive people tend to attribute the good things in life to themselves. In other words, pessimists don't think they cause good things to happen, whereas positive people do. For instance, if a negative thinker receives a pay raise at work, they are unlikely to take any credit for this improvement in their lives. Instead, they may put the change down to a company policy that has little or nothing to do with them. A positive person will be thankful and proud of the fact that they earned a higher wage for doing a job well. In order to think more positively about the events in your life, stop and think about how you made the good things happen. Give yourself the credit you deserve for achieving these things and stop blaming yourself for the bad occurrences you have no control over.

Being more thankful will help you see your life in a more positive light. It's useful to be able to think of what your life would be like without the things you take for granted. Do you have running water? A warm and safe place to sleep? Are you able to feed yourself? It's easy to forget that not everyone has access to these things. Every now and then, it may pay to pause for a moment and consider what your life would be like if you didn't have the things that keep you safe and healthy. Beyond the basics, there's a lot more than you could imagine to be thankful for. Your relationships with family, friends, beloved pets and co-workers are often things we take for granted, until they're gone. Be glad of the loved ones you have near you. You can use gratefulness to turn negativity into positivity.

If you find yourself being overwhelmed by negative thoughts, like regret, try to think of the things in your life that make you happy. Is there a neighbor you like to talk to on your way home, whose smile makes you happy? Do you have a hobby that makes you feel happy and excited? Are you learning a new skill of which you are especially proud? Try to imagine what your life will be like when you start to master that skill. Allow yourself to feel happy or even excited about the future.

Looking at your life and identifying the sources of your negative thoughts and feelings will help you figure out how to fill your life with positivity. Are there certain people or situations that make you feel bad, upset or hurt? You may find your workplace to be negative. A boss or colleague may have a toxic personality. Their treatment of you may be the cause of your negative thoughts, feelings and actions. It may pay to leave your workplace if the climate or individuals are toxic. Finding a job where you are a valued member and where you are treated with respect will boost your self-esteem, make you feel happier and more fulfilled. This in turn will change your negative outlook.

HOW TO ACT AND SPEAK MORE POSITIVELY

If you're in the habit of thinking and feeling down, most likely that's the way you come across to other people. If you are pessimistic this will show in your interactions with other people. Starting to think more positively will help you act more positively, but years of acting and being a certain way may be hard to change. You may need to learn how to act in a positive way on the outside as well as the inside. Here are a few examples of how to project positivity to the world:

- **Body Language.** The way you carry yourself has a big influence on how the world sees you. Standing with shoulders hunched, your eyes down and with a blank expression on your face will make you appear distant, unhappy and unapproachable. Try to open up your body language, instead, to draw people to you. Stand straight with your shoulders back.

This will make you appear confident and open. There are many studies suggesting that smiling is contagious. Smiling and making eye contact will make other people feel happy too. Not only do smiles make you appear happier, there's evidence to suggest smiling fools your own brain into being happier! So, next time you feel a bit blue, try a smile—it may turn your mood around.

- **Speak Optimistically.** Using more positive language will make you sound happier. When you use negative words or phrases it makes you sound less happy and more pessimistic. For instance, try changing "I'm tired" to "I could do with a rest." The original statement sounds a bit defeated and...well...tired. Instead, talking about needing rest is a positive solution that sounds desirable. We could all use a little more rest! Exchange "I forgot" to "I'll set a reminder next time." This small, subtle change doesn't focus on the mistake; it instead focuses on putting in strategy a plan to avoid the mistake in the future.

TIPS FOR BOOSTING YOUR POSITIVITY

1. **Replace negative thoughts with positive ones.** If you feel annoyed that your plans are ruined by a rainy day, try to be glad that the water will nourish your garden. If you feel like you're not getting anywhere in life, grab the moment and decide you have little to lose so make a big change.

2. **Be nice to others, even when they aren't nice to you.** Beyond boosting your karma, being nice makes you feel good. Compliment people who deserve it. There's always something good to say about anyone. Choosing to say nice things to and about people will make you seem and feel positive.

3. **Only expend energy on things you can change or control.** Don't fret about the weather ruining your plans. Make alternate plans. Jump in puddles! Find fun in every situation.

4. **Be excited.** Do you get excited about things? If there are things you love, express that to yourself and others. Get excited about the future. Believe and project your understanding that the future is bright.

5. **Find the humor in things.** Negative situations always feel better if you can laugh. The bad things that happen today often make for a funny story later. Thinking of humor in bad times shows an understanding of the fact that things will get better.

6. **Visualize every step in achieving your goal.** This will make the small, niggly steps seem like big wins. Every time you get a step closer to your goal, you will feel revitalised. Positive visualisation helps you feel optimistic and excited about the future.

7. **Be aware when things are good.** If something goes well or if it goes to plan, be aware and thankful. If you put more energy into being happy about the good things, no matter how small,

and less energy into your negative experiences, positivity will win out! Even if things don't go so well, if you actively feel and celebrate the good, you will feel more positive. When things start to go well, as they usually inevitably do, then you will feel amazing.

CHAPTER SUMMARY

In this chapter, you learned…

- Your health, relationships and success rate are improved by thinking positively.
- There are many ways to think more positively, including learning optimistic thinking and living in the moment.
- There are many tricks to help you act more positively. For example, using positive language makes you feel more positive.
- Boosting positivity is easy when you know a few tricks. For instance, turn negative thoughts into happy thoughts.

In the next chapter you will learn…

- Why it's bad to settle for things that make you unhappy
- How to embrace change in order to be happy

CHAPTER TEN

DON'T SETTLE FOR WHAT MAKES YOU UNHAPPY

We all like to feel safe, and change can be difficult. Even when times are tough, we may be afraid to change our circumstances in case they get even worse. It can be hard to have faith in a new future when you've known a lot of hardship or pain. Even when we haven't had it so bad, it can be difficult to step out of our comfort zone in order to try to make life even better. Why is that? It's because of the unknown; the what ifs. What if I change jobs and find my new job is even worse than my current job? What if I move to a new city and can't find a job or make new friends? What if I move to a new country and end up hating it? What if I end our three-year relationship and can't find anyone else? The list of what ifs is endless. There's another way to look at what ifs, though. For instance, what if I don't make a change for the better? The answer is simple. If you don't make a change, you just stay where you are. Without change we become stagnant. Not changing may mean missing out on making the best decision you ever made.

WHY IT'S BAD TO SETTLE

Settling means continuing with the status quo. It means predictability and stability, both of which are comforting. But settling also means you're missing out on your best life. It can mean you're unhappy in your job, your relationship and your everyday life. Fear can stop us from refusing to settle. We may not even realize we're settling. We may think it's normal to be mildly disappointed every day. But it doesn't have to be that way. You *can* do better than just settling.

Settling for less in romance can lead to arguments, anger, withdrawal and even depression. If you are with someone out of habit, or because being with them supplies you with a sense of stability, then you may end up being miserable in the relationship. If your partner falls short of your expectations, you will inevitably take it out on them. If you end up spending years with the wrong person, you will possibly come to resent them. Years of an unhappy partnership is unhealthy for both people in the relationship. If there are children involved the impact of a negative relationship gets passed onto innocent children.

If you stay in a job that is below your skill level, it can mean you aren't challenged. You are less likely to enjoy your job day to day. Your mental health can be affected with symptoms of depression and anxiety if your job isn't stimulating, interesting or rewarding enough. Given how much time we spend at work, we should try to find a job that we enjoy.

Not all friendships are created equal. You may have a long-term friendship with someone who takes more than they give. Sometimes, we're friends with someone who isn't good for us out of habit or nostalgia. But staying in a toxic friendship can be harmful to our self-esteem, our happiness and our freedom. The friend who takes more than they give will always put themselves first.

It's not just people who can hold us back from reaching our potential. Sometimes the place we live doesn't allow us to be our best. If you've lived in one place for most of your life, it can be scary to think about moving to a new city, or even a new country. But sometimes, the place where we're from doesn't have as much to offer us as it could. For instance, a small, country town will not offer the kinds of jobs you'd be able to find in a big city. Conversely, if what you're after is a quiet country life, on a farm for instance, you're unlikely to find your dream life in the city.

HOW TO EMBRACE CHANGE

The best way to accept change is to understand that it's a part of life. Right from birth, we're thrust into a world that's new. We came from the safe and comfortable environment of our mother's womb into a brand-new world, and from the moment we took our first breath, we've been bombarded with endless new experiences. We're not just used to change. We're experts at change. Children are especially good at dealing with change. It's not just that they have no choice—they can't really avoid changing classes at school each year and moving up the grade. Children are especially good at dealing with change because their thinking is more malleable than that of an adult. In order to deal with change, we can learn from children, who just tend to face change by accepting it and moving on.

So how can we face change with childlike acceptance? Children go along with change because they have to. Most of the time, adults decide things for them and they get used to being thrust into new situations. Because of this, children don't tend to take the situation they're in too personally. They don't tend to worry over whether or not change is going to disrupt their lives the way grown-ups do. In order to accept change, we can also try to consider it as something that's separate from ourselves. The change that is occurring, whether it be moving to a new city or country, changing jobs, or even ending a relationship, needs not define us. Yes, it will alter our lives, sometimes quite a bit, but it doesn't alter who we are. One change, even a big one, doesn't define you. You are the sum of many years of experiences, not just one change.

Accept change by celebrating it. Every time you make a change for the better, you are getting closer to your goals. Every set is worth celebrating. Take time to acknowledge how strong you are in embarking on every change you make. Sometimes when we make a change, we expect life to improve instantly. This is not always the case. Sometimes, it takes a while for us to reap the rewards of taking a new path. So, even if it doesn't immediately feel like the shift you've made in your life is for the better, have the optimism and belief that it will serve you well in the end.

HOW TO EMBRACE CHANGE

Don't ignore the feelings that change brings about. Change can cause us to feel many emotions, and that's natural. If we name these emotions caused by change, we can learn to accept the situation we're in. Try to list the emotions you feel when you are going through a change in your life, below are a few examples:

1. Nervous
2. Excited

3. Disappointed
4. In Shock
5. Confused
6. Overwhelmed
7. Relieved
8. Empty

There are many emotions that come with change. Sometimes we may feel excited by change. If we have a new job, it can be exciting going in on your first day, anticipating how it's going to be. Other times we can feel disappointed. We may have dreamed of doing something and built it up in our minds. When we finally make the change, it may not live up to our expectations. For instance, moving to a new city may not turn out to be as exciting as you anticipated. This disappointment may leave us feeling empty. It's good to name all of these emotions instead of ignoring them. By naming the emotions, we can do something about them. If we're disappointed by change, we can try to come up with solutions. If we're disappointed about moving to a new city, we may need to figure out whether the feeling is just temporary. In other words, it takes time to adjust when it comes to change. Once a routine is established and we start to feel more comfortable, then we can figure out how to make the best of the new situation we are in. In the case of moving to a new city, we can try to identify why we're feeling disappointed. It might be that we feel lonely in a new city having left our old friends behind. In this case, you can do something about it. You could try to form new friendships by picking up a hobby, joining a club, or putting yourself in situations where you might meet people.

Fear is one of the most common reactions to change. We often respond to fear with a fight or flight response. That is, we will either try to fight the situation or flee from it. Fleeing change means we will try to avoid it, perhaps by going back to a situation we were in before. So, if we've left a long-term partner who isn't good for us we may flee the change by going back to our partner, even if this isn't good for us. Fighting change means we may try to go against change. For instance, let's say you decided to become a parent. When this change occurs, fear might make you want to avoid the reality of what's happening. You may try to evade responsibility by taking on extra hours at work to stay away from home. Instead of giving in to fight or flight, try to stop and think before you act. Instead of running back to your ex-partner out of fear, take a moment to remember why you left them in the first place. Going back to an unhealthy relationship won't solve the problem of feeling lonely. It will just make you more unhappy. If you fear the responsibility of parenthood, try to take it a day at a time. Some change feels so overwhelming because of the long-term commitment it represents. Instead of looking at parenthood as something that will tie you down for a large part of your life, try to consider each day as it comes.

Change can offer you new possibilities. Sometimes we stagnate in life, doing the same thing and getting nowhere. Change is the one thing out of which new possibilities can emerge. If you find yourself without a job, it may lead you to consider doing further study. This study might take you in a completely different direction. This new direction might turn out to be the best thing that ever happened to you! Without the original change (losing your job), you wouldn't have discovered the thing you were meant to do.

Whether you make the change yourself, or whether change happens to you, how you react to it can determine your future. The way to ensure that change works in your favor is to try to make the best of it. Here are some tips and tricks to help you take advantage of change:

- **Broaden your horizons.** Use change as a chance to try something you've always wanted to do. Let's say you've become redundant. You could try to find another job in the same area, or you could try to go in a completely different direction. Perhaps you could start your own business. You could seek further education to upgrade your skills in order to progress further in your chosen field, or to specialize or upgrade. For example, if you've trained and worked as a veterinary nurse but would like to take on more responsibility, you could train to become a veterinary surgeon.

- **Let change open up new doors for you.** You never know where change may lead you. Meeting new people and going to new places may give you new opportunities. For example, if you decide to take on a new hobby or join a volunteer organisation you will meet people from different backgrounds. These people may be able to introduce you to opportunities you would not have been offered otherwise. A new friend may happen to be looking for someone to work for them and they'll be more likely to offer a job to someone they know than a stranger. You could end up finding the love of your life when you change jobs, move to a new city or join a new club or group. If your life stayed the same, you may have missed the chance to fall in love!

- **Allow change to change you, as well.** You might learn exciting new things about yourself when you are in a different situation. You may think of yourself as a quiet person who doesn't get on well with people in groups. However, if you find a hobby or sport that you enjoy you may find yourself being able to communicate more effectively in a crowd. When you play a sport or hobby this becomes a shared interest among the people you do this with which allows you to open up to them. Through this shared interest you will likely learn how to talk to people about a broader range of topics.

CHAPTER SUMMARY

In this chapter, you learned...

- There are many examples for why it's bad to settle, including missing out on opportunities and being unhappy in your job and other areas of life
- Embrace change by understanding it is part of life and learn to go with the emotions involved

In the next chapter, you will learn...

- How to figure out if you have healthy work environment
- How to figure out if you have a healthy friendship environment
- How to figure out if you have a healthy romantic environment
- Whether the environment you live in is best for you

CHAPTER ELEVEN

CREATE ENVIRONMENTS YOU CAN THRIVE IN

Humans are social animals. We're deeply affected by our interpersonal relationships. How we interact with people on a daily basis can have a big effect on our moods, mental health, wellbeing, and self-esteem. The people in our lives make up part of our environment, shaping our lives every bit as much as our physical surroundings do. In order to be happy and successful we need to ensure our environment is a healthy one. If the people who we interact with in different environments respect us and influence our lives positively, we will flourish. Conversely, if the people in our environment drag us down and hurt us, we will not be able to succeed.

CREATING A HEALTHY WORK ENVIRONMENT

There are some basic signs that your workplace is a healthy one. If your workplace falls short of many or most of these things, it's a sign your environment is not the best for you.

1. **Your co-workers are trustworthy.** Do you trust your co-workers, supervisors and bosses? Do you feel like they come

through with their promises? If your boss tells you that you will earn a raise if you reach a certain target or perform to a certain standard, do you feel like they will follow through and reward you for your effort as promised.

2. **Is there good communication in your workplace?** Do you feel like you can talk to your co-workers and bosses when you have a problem on the job? If you're struggling do you feel heard or ignored? Does your boss communicate their needs clearly? Are instructions clear and easy to follow, or do you often feel like you have to figure things out as you go?

3. **Does your workplace prioritise your welfare?** Do you feel like you are given emotional support when you need it? A good workplace will try to ensure the work environment is healthy and will foster growth and betterment. A sign of a workplace that cares about its employees is that it will do things to improve their workers' mental and physical health. For instance, they may provide vaccinations, healthy food options, free eye checks and health insurance. They may also invest in your growth by offering additional training and skills so that you have the chance of progressing in your workplace.

4. **Do you feel empowered in your workplace?** Empowering workplaces will reward employees for improvement and growth. If employees feel like their improvement in the workplace will be rewarded, they will feel in control of their situation. Employees feel empowered by the ability to learn with clear instructions. They should also not be made to feel

harshly punished for failure or mistakes. Employees should be given clear guidance about what's expected of them. When they haven't met expectations, employees should be told in a constructive way so they can learn and improve. If you find that you haven't been taught your job properly, which leads to mistakes, this is a sign you haven't been empowered by your workplace. Even worse if you then get reprimanded for this mistake, this is a definite sign that your workplace is not helping you succeed.

5. **Good workplaces will make their employees feel appreciated.** Beyond a weekly pay check, there are many ways an employer can make you feel like your efforts mean something. Bonuses, employee of the month awards, and certificates are a few examples of how an employer might show their gratitude for your efforts. Even if an employer gives out these rewards, a simple "thank you" that is heartfelt and honest sometimes means even more. If your boss or supervisor never thanks you or congratulates your achievements, it may be a sign they don't value you.

6. **Good values are a sign of a healthy workplace.** If your workplace has a mission statement that commits to doing the best for their clients, shareholders, and workers, this is a good start. Do you feel like your workplace as a whole and your bosses and supervisors have your best interests at heart or do you feel like another cog in the wheel? Does your workplace care more about making money than it cares about the environment, it's people and customers?

CREATING A HEALTHY FRIENDSHIP ENVIRONMENT

Really good friendships are rare. The best kind of friend is one who is your equal. They are as interested in you as you are in them. Sometimes we have a few friends who are close and others who are just acquaintances. Other times we have friends who mean a lot to us, but we're not always sure if they truly care about us.

HOW TO TELL IF YOUR FRIENDSHIP IS HEALTHY

- **Your friend listens when you talk.** Some friends talk at length about themselves but they hardly listen when it's your turn to talk.

- **Your friend respects your boundaries.** Having limits to your friendship is important. Boundaries don't mean you are holding your friend at arm's length. It means you have a reciprocal relationship of respect in which you both care about each other's limitations. Strangers or acquaintances may push our boundaries because they don't know us very well, or because the relationship is a polite one in which we feel less inclined to stand up for ourselves. True close friends should know your boundaries and should not push them too far. You may not be much of a hugger, or you may not want to be touched or to shake hands. A close friend will respect these boundaries whereas a stranger might try to shake your hand or hug you.

- **Your friendship is equal in give and take.** Good friends will give and take in equal measure. If you need something from a good friend, they should be willing to give that to you if they are able. Conversely, if your friend needs something from you, they should feel free to ask and receive. For instance, if a friend constantly asks for money for dinner but doesn't ever pay for your meals, then they are more of a taker than a giver.

- **You feel good about yourself when around your friend.** A good friend will build you up by encouraging you and praising you when you've done well. A less positive friend might criticize everything from your fashion sense to your finances in a way that makes you feel bad about yourself. Even if this is done in a way that is meant to be humorous, if it degrades your self-esteem, it's not healthy. A good friend will give you sound advice that will help you overcome obstacles and problems.

- **A good friend likes you for who you are.** If your friend spends a lot of time trying to change you, even if it's "for your own good," it may mean they don't like you for who you are. Advising on your fashion sense or hairstyle is one thing, but if a friend wants you to change your personality or your beliefs, then they don't accept you for who you are.

- **Your friend should make you feel safe.** Friends look out for each other. Sometimes even good friends will gossip, but if your friend can't be trusted with important private details about your life, it's hard for you to feel safe around them. The friend who is always telling tales behind your back, distorting the truth about you, is not a safe friend.

- **A good friend is your cheerleader.** They will root for you and fight in your corner as you strive for your goals and ambitions.

It can be hard to decide whether or not to cut ties with a friend. There's probably a good reason the two of you chose to spend time together. You probably have shared interests, you most likely get along well and have a shared history together. The positive things about your relationship will be difficult to turn your back on. However, if your friendship isn't positive it might be best for your wellbeing to cut ties. How do you decide whether to end your friendship with someone you care about? It's not easy. You have to decide whether the positive aspects of your friendship make the negative side worth it. If there's a chance that your friend might change their behavior, it may be worth talking to them and setting some boundaries around their behavior. Give them the chance to change and if the problems continue, then you can decide whether to walk away.

ENDING TOXIC FRIENDSHIPS

There's a difference between a friend who occasionally steps over the boundaries, or who can be a little self-centred, and a friend who is toxic and harmful. You will have to make the decision yourself about whether or not your friend's negative behavior has gone too far.

Examples of toxic/harmful traits include backstabbing and lying behind your back, stealing, demeaning and making fun in a spiteful way, trying to outdo you, putting you down, dominating you and leading you astray, gaslighting, passive aggressive behavior, and bullying.

It can sometimes be hard to know if your friend is being humorous when they make fun of you. Some people show their affection for people they care about by making fun of them. If your friend makes fun of you in a way that is hurtful, letting them know how you feel should put an end to the behavior. If they ignore your wishes and continue to make fun of you, it may mean they aren't the right friend for you.

BEING HEALTHY IN LOVE

The attributes of a good relationship with the person we fall in love with are similar to that of a close friend. As with positive friendships, romantic relationships should have positive traits like trust, openness, good communication and more. Romantic relationships also have a deeper level of intimacy that is both emotional and physical. Romance and intimacy can make relationships more difficult to judge than friendship. Physical attraction can be so strong and the emotional connection so deep that we tend to forgive our romantic partners for things that we would never allow a platonic friend to get away with. As with friendships, it's important for us to know what our boundaries and limits are when it comes to the one we love.

TRAITS OF A HEALTHY ROMANTIC RELATIONSHIP

Acceptance is one of the most important traits of a successful romantic relationship. However, if one partner continuously seeks to change the other in some way, this can cause tension and a low self-esteem. So, if there's something your partner does or says that you find annoying, how do you address it without being controlling or judgmental? The best way to approach your differences is to be open and honest. Telling your partner how you feel and asking them to change is reasonable. However, if they can't or won't make the change, you shouldn't try to force them to change or try to control their behavior. If your partner tries to change you using force or by controlling you, this is not healthy.

The cornerstone of every healthy partnership is equality. No matter which sex you are in the partnership and regardless of your working status or your caregiving role, you should not feel like you are less than your partner. In the past, women were seen as inferior to their husbands, who were considered to be more important because they were the ones making the money and "putting bread on the table," so to speak. These days, the roles of stay-at-home parents (of any sex) should be considered equally important. There are many ways one person in the partnership can be made to feel unequal. Having less control over finances can place one of you in an inferior position, making that partner more dependent. If one person controls the money it makes the other more dependent on them. These days men and women both tend to work, but, due to old fashioned ideas, the woman sometimes ends up doing more housework than the male. If you both work there's no reason why you both can't share chores and errands. If a relationship isn't equal then it can lead to feelings of resentment, disempowerment and, eventually, anger and frustration. If one partner puts more into a relationship, whether it be in terms of money, time, effort, or even care and attention, then they will feel used and unappreciated. In fact, many studies show that inequality in marriage makes divorce more likely to occur. For instance, studies show that women who do a disproportionate amount of housework are described as being less satisfied in their marriage and are more likely to seek a divorce.

Communication is as important in romance as it is with other relationships. You should feel able to express yourself to your partner without feeling judged. If you find yourself having endless disagreements that don't resolve and just continue to go around and around, it may be a sign that you are not well matched. If your relationship has a lot of friction, it may mean one or both of you needs to learn how to communicate more effectively. One or both of you may even need anger management therapy. Sometimes, the inability to communicate in a relationship stems from childhood issues like abuse or childhood psychological disorders. In other words, anger and argumentativeness may not be you or your partner's fault. Seeking counselling may help you fix the communication problems in your relationship. If, however, counselling and therapy don't help, it may mean the relationship is not good for you.

CHAPTER SUMMARY

In this chapter, you learned...

- Signs of an unhealthy work environment include bad communication and untrustworthy colleagues. Decide whether or not to stay in a job based on the health of the environment.
- Choose whether to stay in a friendship depending on whether it's a healthy one. For instance, if your friend listens and refrains from talking behind your back, it's a good sign you have a healthy friendship
- Choose to stay in a healthy relationship or to leave it depending on whether or not it's healthy. For instance, if you argue a lot and don't spend time together, it's a sign to seek counselling or move on.

In the next chapter, you will learn...

- That it's okay to say no
- Tips to help you say no more often
- How saying yes too often can be worse than saying no
- How saying no can actually be a good thing

CHAPTER TWELVE

LEARNING HOW TO SAY NO

We weren't allowed to say no to our parents when we were children. We had to do what our teachers asked us to do without question. We weren't allowed to talk back or act as if we weren't happy to do what we were told. Then, suddenly, as adults we're supposed to be able to make up our own minds about whether or not we want to do as we're asked. Or are we? How many times have you said no to your boss in the workplace?

It's not just that we've been taught to say yes to anyone who is in a position of authority over us, we're also programmed to be helpful to other people. It's hard for us to say no because it's not polite to deny people. It's hard to say no for a number of reasons. We may not want to hurt someone's feelings. We may not want to let someone down. We may also fear being rejected or judged or even angering someone.

Of course, it feels good to be able to help people. Helping others is good for your own mental health and wellbeing. But there is such a thing as being *too* helpful. If you simply can't say no, no matter how busy you are, this goes beyond being helpful. You're actually putting others ahead of yourself. Saying yes can be so automatic that you don't even think about it before you agree to something. This sort of willingness can not only oblige you to do more than you have the time or inclination for, it can sometimes go against your values. What if someone asks you to do something that you don't quite agree with. For instance, someone might ask you to lie for them. If you're an honest person, this might go against your morals.

The number one thing you should remember about saying yes is that you aren't obliged to agree to anything you don't want to do, and you don't have to agree to do anything you don't have the time for.

IT'S OKAY TO SAY NO

If you've spent most of your life saying yes, it can be difficult to figure out how to say no. Here are some tips to help you learn how to turn someone down:

- **Don't say yes immediately.** Try to give yourself a little time before you answer. Tell someone, "I'll get back to you" or "I'll let you know tomorrow." This way, you have a moment to think before you decide whether their request is something you want to do. If you are a yes person, you're likely to say yes instantly. Telling people, you'll get back to them gives you the chance to think over their request. It also gives them the idea that there is a hint that their request might not be something you're comfortable with.

- **Try to think of your denial as a refusal and not something personal.** You're not rejecting or denying the individual for personal reasons. It doesn't mean you think less of them or that you're trying to hurt or deny them. You are saying no to a situation, not a person.

- **Keep it simple.** Your response doesn't need to be long or complicated. You don't need to supply a list of reasons. You don't have to convince anyone that you can't do something. Be polite, but succinct and clear. Try a response that conveys regret but that is also a clear refusal. For instance, you could say, "Thanks for thinking of me, but I'm afraid I'm not available right now."

- **Try to come to a compromise.** If the request is something you would be happy to do if it weren't inconvenient, you could suggest fulfilling part of their request, doing so at a later date, or swapping jobs/tasks with them.

- **Don't make excuses.** If you don't want to do something, you are allowed to say no. You shouldn't have to make up an excuse. If you do, you haven't got the message across and you will be asked the same thing again in the future. It's best to bite the bullet and say no the first time.

HOW SAYING YES CAN CAUSE MORE BAD THAN GOOD

Saying yes when you don't want to do something can be worse than saying no. Resentment can build when you find yourself putting in time and effort for something you'd rather not be doing. You can end up missing out on doing the things you need to do. You can fall behind on your work or in other areas of your social life. You might end up letting down other people in your life who rely on you. For instance, if you continually agree to do extra hours in order to please your boss, you might be letting your family down. Overworking can result in missing out on family events and milestones. Your partner will resent you because they are doing your share of the caregiving and you will miss out on spending quality time with you children who may grow up feeling unvalued as a result.

If you say yes to everything whenever anyone asks for help you'll end up stretching yourself too thin. You won't be able to do a good job at work, home or in any other area of your life. You need to learn to prioritize. The only way to do that is to say no sometimes.

HOW SAYING NO CAN BE GOOD

Sometimes saying no does more good than bad. Here are a few examples of how saying no makes life better:

1. **People will respect you more if you have boundaries.** If you offer up your time and energy freely people don't value you as much. If you say no, for good reason, they will realize your time is important. They may start to respect you more in other areas of your life as well.

2. **People may start to take advantage if you say yes, all the time.** If someone knows you'll say yes, they may ask for your

help even when they don't really need it. They may essentially turn you into their servant, making you run around after them.

3. **Help others become more independent.** If people in your life constantly take advantage of your helpful nature, it can mean they don't learn to stand on their own two feet. By denying them your help occasionally, you are helping them to become more independent.

4. **People will be more thankful when you do agree to help them.** If you say yes all of the time, people will get used to your help and they will take it for granted. They will take your help as a given, instead of a favor for which they should be grateful.

5. **Saying no means, you're putting yourself first.** Saying no is an important part of self-care. You need to put yourself first, sometimes. If you have plans, you shouldn't feel obliged to change them for someone else. If all you do is give to others, you will feel drained emotionally and physically. Often, the most important person you need to help is yourself! You are just as important as anyone else.

6. **Saying no shows others that you respect yourself.** Seeing your own time as important shows other people that you see yourself as important. Saying no also means you respect other people enough to tell them how you really feel. It shows them that you feel your relationship is strong enough for you to be real. This will strengthen your relationship, not weaken it,

because it means your relationship is based one something deeper than favors. It's based on friendship, not usefulness.

7. **You get to do what you want if you say no to other people.** This means you can have more "me time." Or you have more time to spend with family and friends. You may be able to put more effort into your career or business if you don't give away too much of your time to others.

8. **Saying no reduces your stress.** If you struggle to meet everyone else's needs, it can be difficult to succeed in your own life. You can end up burnt out and anxious because you're struggling to fit everything in. We're aware, on a subconscious level, when we give more in a relationship than the other person does. It can cause hurt feelings if we are always the one who's giving. We feel more like a commodity than a friend if we're only valued for what we can do for other people.

9. **People will learn to like you for who you are, rather than what you can do.** If you say no every now and then, people may start to see you differently. They may start to value you for the person you are. If, on the other hand, saying no makes the other person withdraw their friendship, it's a sign they weren't truly your friend to begin with. Saying no is a good way to find out who your real friends are. Learning that your friends are just using you and that it's not you that they really care about may be hurtful for a while, but you'll be better off in the long run.

CHAPTER SUMMARY

In this chapter, you learned...

- There are many things you can try to make saying no easier. For instance, delay saying yes so, the refusal isn't so blunt.
- Saying yes can be worse than saying no. For example, saying yes too often means people will get used to it and take advantage.
- Saying no can be good. For instance, people will respect you more and will be more thankful when you do say yes.

In the next chapter, you will learn...

- How to live a balanced life
- How exercise will help you lead a more balanced life
- How eating well will make you lead a better life

CHAPTER THIRTEEN

PRACTICE SELF-COMPASSION

We spend a lot of time caring about other people. We tend to put the people who depend on us first. If we have elderly parents, we do everything we can to make sure their needs are met. If we have young children, we put in a lot of time, effort and sacrifice to make sure they get everything they need. Our siblings and friends, neighbors, clients and even strangers may also need our help. By the time we've finished taking care of everyone else, we have little time and energy to think of ourselves. The result can often be that we're the ones who end up feeling stressed, exhausted and strung out. Taking care of everyone else often means we put ourselves last most of the time. The demand of balancing a career with family obligations can mean that we can end up being the one who needs help! You can't put yourself last indefinitely. In the end, neglecting your self-care will catch up with you, and your physical and mental health will suffer. You've done so much for everyone else. Now, it's time to take care of the most important person in your life: you.

MIND-BODY CONNECTION

The mind-body connection means that the thoughts, feelings and sensations we have can affect our bodies. How we think, feel and act can affect our health. In recent years, the effects of our mind on our bodies have been shown scientifically. For instance, the sensation of stress has been seen to have a negative effect on white blood cells. In other words, as white blood cells are responsible for fighting infection, stress can lower our immunity. If you are unable to manage your stress levels, this can have an effect on how well your body fights infection. To make sure you can remain fit and healthy, you must find a way to keep your stress levels under control.

STRIKE A BALANCE

One way to keep your stress levels from rising is to make sure you maintain a healthy work-life balance. If you work too much, neglecting the other areas of your life your mind-body connection will become out of sync. Even if you love your job, too much work equals too much stress, which will negatively impact your health. Striking a healthy work-life balance is crucial to your ability to function properly. For a more balanced life, make sure you make time to meet your social needs, as well. Meet with friends and loved ones in order to make sure your social needs are met. To make sure your physical and mental health is in balance, make time for yourself. We've already discussed the importance of 'me time' and the need to strike a life balance is one of the reasons why it's important to give yourself some down time. Don't feel bad about pampering yourself. It's crucial to your life balance. So, next time you're at the beauty spa getting a massage don't think of it as spoiling yourself. Think of it as a crucial part of maintaining a balanced life!

EXERCISE TO FEEL GOOD

Exercising has benefits beyond losing weight and getting fit. Exercise is a good way to reduce stress as it helps you expel excess frustration and energy. Exercise has been shown to reduce stress hormones in the body (e.g. cortisol and adrenaline). It also releases endorphins (the feel-good chemicals that make you happy). If you choose the right form of exercise, not only will you decrease stress levels, you'll also have fun. Choose an exercise that will make you happy. If you love lifting weights, the gym is probably for you. But if you find hefting weights around a chore, perhaps it's best to find something you're likely to get a kick out of. Try horseback riding, swimming or skiing. Be adventurous and try something new that you've always wanted to do.

EAT HEALTHY COMFORT FOOD

It's easy to seek comfort in unhealthy food, especially when we're busy or stressed. But it's well worth taking time to prepare a healthy, home-cooked meal instead of stopping at a fast food joint. Healthy food will nurture your body with good vitamins and minerals. A balanced diet is as good for the mind as it is for the body. Studies show fast foods increase physical health problems like diabetes and heart disease. But unhealthy food can also affect the mind in a negative way. One study showed that people who ate a more healthy Mediterranean diet, as opposed to a high fat western diet, were 35% less likely to suffer from depression. Eat well and you will look and feel so much better.

To recover from the daily stress of work and everyday life, you need a good night of sleep. It can be hard to turn off our brains after a hectic day. In order to help you relax and reap the benefit of a deep, uninterrupted sleep try to prepare your body with a relaxing sleep routine. Try drinking a hot, non-caffeinated beverage before bedtime, warm milk or camomile tea, known for their calming qualities, are good choices. It's great if reading helps to put you in a sleepy mood, but try to avoid reading from an electronic device, or use a blue light blocker to prevent blue light from keeping you awake. After reading until you feel sleepy, try some mindfulness breathing exercises or practice meditation in order to bring you to a deeper level of relaxation.

CHAPTER SUMMARY

In this chapter, you learned...

- You can live a balanced life by striking a balance between work and play by meeting social, physical and friendship needs
- Balance your life by exercising in order to feel good
- Make life better by eating well

In the next chapter, you will learn...

- How to act in order to take control of your life
- How to show love, respect and kindness to others

CHAPTER FOURTEEN

TAKE CONTROL OF YOUR LIFE

You don't have to be a passenger in your own life. You can take control of the direction you want to go. You don't have to settle for a job that makes you miserable. You don't have to stay in any situation that makes you feel like a failure. In order to be who, you want to be, you have to take control of your own life.

TAKE ACTION

Now that you know about showing self-compassion and having a positive mindset, it's time to put these concepts into action. Having a positive mindset will help you achieve your goals. If you're positive it shows: you appear more confident, charismatic and in control. You will also feel more energized if you think you're going to succeed at something. Fearing failure, or thinking the odds are low of achieving something will sap your energy. Like a self-fulfilling prophecy, having a negative mindset will be more likely to bring about a negative result.

Here are a few positive ways to take action:

1. **Start your day by doing the most difficult thing.** Getting the hardest task done straight away means you won't be worried or

nervous about it throughout the day. If the first thing you do is achieve the most difficult thing on your to-do list, you will set yourself up with positivity for the day.

2. **Don't wait until later.** If the task at hand seems monumental, don't be discouraged as this can lead to procrastination. Try breaking big tasks down into smaller parts. If you set smaller goals, you will feel pleased with your achievement, which will spur you on to the next mini task. Before you know it, the task will be complete! Instead of feeling proud of one single achievement, you'll feel happy at having achieved lots of smaller goals, which will give you a confidence boost throughout the day.

3. **Take a break.** It's easy to feel overwhelmed if you have a lot on your plate, or if you're dealing with something important. Show self-compassion by scheduling regular breaks. Even if what you're dealing with seems time-sensitive, grabbing five minutes of "me time" is something you should do. Once you've had a break, you'll be able to think more clearly and work more efficiently. So, think of taking a breather as a way to increase the likelihood of success.

4. **Stay positive.** Show self-compassion by cutting yourself some slack. If a goal seems to be going badly, don't allow yourself to feel like a failure. Try to look at the bigger picture. You have a lifetime to get things right. One small hurdle won't break you. Know you'll do better next time.

5. **Be brave.** It can be hard to try new things. Going outside of your comfort zone can be intimidating. Taking on a new job, moving to a different country, starting a business, all of these things carry risk of failure. But if you don't give new things a go you may live to regret the chance you didn't take. Be positive, be brave and take a leap every now and then.

6. **Try something new often.** If you broaden your horizons, you will experience new surroundings, new people, new adventures and new ideas. You will be changed and inspired by learning new things and meeting new people. Going somewhere new and meeting different people can open doors for you. You never know where life can take you if you open the door to new experiences.

SHOWING LOVE, RESPECT AND KINDNESS FOR OTHERS

So far, we've talked about treating yourself with compassion and love. But in order to be happy, it's important for you to extend the same kindness to others. If you treat others well, they will usually treat you well in return. Being kind to others has a positive effect on our own lives. We feel better about ourselves when we are kind. We get a sense of pride and wellbeing out of going the extra mile for others. The following tips can help get you started:

- **Empathize with others.** Expressing empathy is one of the most loving things we can do for others. Empathy is one step further than showing sympathy. It means we have tried to put ourselves in another person's shoes to truly feel what they are going through. Having empathy for someone allows for a deeper connection. If you show empathy for others, they are more likely to try to see things from your point of view, too.

- **Be supportive.** Letting someone know you are there for them is one of the most valuable gifts you can offer. Being available when needed is the best way to show someone you care. If you show someone how important they are by being there for them, they are more likely to do the same for you.

- **Be humble.** This includes apologizing to the other person; to say you're sorry is a form of love because you are putting another person's feelings ahead of your pride and shame. We all make mistakes. Owning up to mistakes will show others that you're aware of the hurt you've caused and that their feelings are important to you.

- **Make time for someone else.** Giving your time is a great way to show love for someone. We're all busy and tend to rely on texting and social media to check in with someone. A visit in person or a phone call can cheer someone up and make their day. They'll know how much you care if you take time out of your busy day for them. If you make time for others, they will be more available for you when you need them.

- **Forgive their mistakes.** Forgiveness is perhaps the greatest display of loving others that you can express. If someone has hurt you, being able to forgive them may be difficult, if not impossible. Holding onto a grudge can be bad for you. If you can forgive someone you will be free of heartache and anger. If you behave in a forgiving way in your everyday life, others will also be more forgiving of your mistakes.

TIPS FOR SHOWING RESPECT TO OTHERS

- **Tell the truth.** Being honest can be difficult. We may be reluctant to tell the truth in case we hurt or anger someone. Trusting your relationship with someone enough to weather honesty is a sign of respect. It means you trust the other person to handle the way things really are.

- **Be polite.** We're all taught to be polite from a young age. Sometimes, when we're in a hurry or frustrated, we can forget our manners. It's in these moments that it's most important for us to remember to respect others by being polite. If we show politeness to others even when we're stressed and annoyed, they will treat us with the same respect.

- **Listen to what they have to say.** Active listening is a way of showing people that you respect their opinions. When you talk to people, make sure to take a real interest in what they are saying. Don't just gloss over their point of view in order to get to what you want to say. If you're present and really listening when they talk, they will be more likely to listen and hear you when you speak.

- **Respect other people's personal space.** This is a great way of showing you care about their boundaries. Everyone has a different idea of what personal space means. For some, standing too close to someone is too much. Other people may get so close they're touching. They may frequently hug others, lean on them and touch them. It's important to try to figure out other people's physical space limits and to respect them. People will appreciate it if you care enough to notice when they're uncomfortable.

- **Respect the differences of others.** Though this is sometimes difficult since you may disagree with someone and even feel upset about their point of view, you can still respect someone who has a different opinion than you do by remaining polite and calm. Don't get angry and try to keep an open mind. If you can show respect for people whose opinions are different from your own, they will grant you the same courtesy.

TIPS FOR SHOWING KINDNESS TO OTHERS

- **Lift someone's spirits.** This is a simple kindness that can make a big difference in someone's life. It doesn't cost you much to give someone a compliment, but it might just make their day. If you go out of your way to make people feel good, not only will you be rewarded by the feeling of being responsible for other's happiness, people will also be kinder to you.

- **Small acts of kindness can go a long way.** A kind act which isn't difficult for you to do can help others a great deal. For instance, giving a few dollars to someone who has nothing can mean the difference between a meal and going hungry for them. Spending a few extra minutes chatting to an elderly neighbor may not seem significant to you, but to a lonely neighbor, their entire day has just been made so much brighter.

- **Pay it forward.** Generosity is a nice way to spread kindness. If you pass down some unwanted clothes to a family in need, not only have you helped them through tough times, you've also increased the likelihood that they will do the same for others when they are in a better position. You never know when you may need help. One day, kindness to another may come back to you when you need it the most.

- **Constructive criticism.** If someone does a bad job, or makes a mistake, think of it as a teaching moment. Try to help someone improve if they haven't met your expectations. If you get angry or put them down, they will lose confidence and make more mistakes. If you go easy on other people they may cut you some slack in return. For instance, if you find yourself being served by a clumsy waitress at a restaurant, don't get angry, encourage them to do better next time.

Go out of your way to help others and they may take a leaf out of your book and do the same. Spread kindness through your actions and make your world a better place.

CHAPTER SUMMARY

In this chapter, you learned…

- Actively take control of your life in a number of ways, such as breaking tasks into smaller pieces
- Show love, kindness, and respect for others in as many ways as you can, such as by lifting people's spirits, small acts of kindness, and more

In the next chapter, you will learn…

- 10 mindfulness meditations to try

CHAPTER FIFTEEN

10 MINDFULNESS MEDITATIONS TO TRY

Mediation has so many benefits for your wellbeing. Meditation has an amazing calming effect, and there are few other things that can help relax you for sleep. Meditation will also improve your ability to focus. Meditation helps you to focus on one thing, be that your breathing, sounds around you, or other methods of attaining a deeper state of consciousness. This focus will block out negative thoughts, it will decrease your anxiety and help improve your overall mood. If you can learn to calm your mind, slow your breathing, and stop your mind from racing, you have effectively learned how to regulate your mood through meditation. You will be able to control emotional outbursts. As you practice meditation, you will quickly be able to bring yourself to a state of peace within minutes of practice. Once you become adept at meditation, you should be able to practice it anywhere, no matter how stressed you are or how hectic your environment is.

TYPES OF MEDITATION

Body Scan Meditation: After sitting or lying down in a comfortable position, scan your entire body from your toes all the way up to the top of your head. Starting at your toes, take note of how they feel, are they warm, cold, stiff, or sore? Work your way up your body, taking note of your feet, up to your ankles, your calves, knees and so forth until you reach the top of your head. If you've made sure to concentrate on each body part taking your mind off all other distractions you will be able to reach a deep level of calm and relaxation.

Muscle Tension Meditation: Repeat the body scan as before but this time squeeze each body part holding the squeeze for a few seconds before moving on to the next body part. This is a good meditation to try if you find it difficult to concentrate when doing a simple body scan. The contrast between squeezing and releasing will enable you to relax more deeply.

Counting Meditation: Counting is used as a way of taking your mind away from distractions. Try to empty your mind of all thoughts and feelings and begin to count backward from one hundred. Try to block out any sounds of sensations around you. If you find simple subtraction is too easy, try subtracting by multiples of two. For example, if you begin with the number 100, subtract by 2 to get 98, and then subtract by 2 again to get 96 and so forth. Keep going until you feel deeply relaxed. You may find yourself falling asleep as you subtract. That's perfectly normal and is a sign that the meditation is working well! If you're a bit of a math whizz try subtracting by larger numbers like 4.

Sound Meditation: Close your eyes and begin by listening to the sounds that you can hear close by. Concentrate on what you can hear in the room near you, like the creaking of the floor or the vibration of the refrigerator. Push your hearing further to just beyond the window. Listen for outside sounds nearby, like the chirping of birds. Let your hearing reach out even further to the sounds of cars going by, airplanes and far off traffic. The concentration it takes to focus on individual sounds will help block out distractions and help you relax.

Deep Breathing Meditation: Lay down flat and place your hand on your stomach as you take a deep breath. Count slowly until you can no longer hold your breath in. Hold your breath for a beat before you begin to slowly let your breath out again counting as you go. Try to inflate the lower part of your lungs by feeling your stomach rise. With practice, you will be able to count your breaths in and out for longer allowing you to reach a deeper level of relaxation. You will also improve your breathing and allow your body to reach deeper oxygenation which will improve your overall health and energy.

Guided Meditation: If you find it difficult to relax while meditating on your own, guided meditation may be your best option. Instead of having to take yourself through the step, with guided meditation, all you need to do is sit or lay back and follow someone else's guidance. There are a variety of guided meditation apps or recordings you can try. You can also take guided meditation classes in person.

Kindness Meditation: This is one of the most rewarding and positive kinds of meditation. In this meditation the object is to send out kindness to the world. Send positive thoughts or and kindness outward to the world in general or to specific people, pets, nations or places. The benefit of sending out kindness is that it fills you with a sense of wellbeing that is rewarding and makes you feel good about yourself.

Transcendental Meditation: This meditation allows you to transcend or improve your state of being through mantra. Mantra involves repeating a saying over and over while relaxing and breathing deeply. You may choose a mantra yourself or use one from your instructor. Something like "I will be kinder to people" would work. You might like to repeat, "I will be kinder to myself," as a reminder to love yourself.

Visualisation Meditation: Begin this meditation by choosing something to visualise. The object in question isn't important. It could be an apple, the sky or a river. Try to visualize every detail about the object. For instance, if the object you've chosen is an apple, try to picture everything you can about it. Think of the color of the skin and any bumps or imperfections on the surface. After that you can think of other sensations like the feel of it. By activating specific parts of the brain, this mediation frees up the rest of your brain, enabling your mind to relax.

Sound Bath Meditation: In this mediation a specific sound is used to trigger relaxation which can be done in person or via a recording. Commonly used sounds for this meditation include gongs and bowls which are tapped or struck to create uniquely relaxing sounds. The more often you meditate to the chosen sounds, the more deeply you will relax as your mind comes to associate the "sound bath" with relaxation.

It doesn't matter which meditation you chose as long as it works for you!

CHAPTER SUMMARY

In this chapter, you learned...

- 10 types of meditation techniques that will help you relax, destress, and practice mindfulness
- In the next chapter, you will learn...
- 40+ "love yourself" quotes

CHAPTER SIXTEEN

40+ LOVE YOURSELF QUOTES

1. How you treat yourself lays the foundations for how others will treat you.

2. No one deserves your love, respect and kindness more than you do.

3. There's only one of you, which means you are rare.

4. You are not your mistakes. Your mistakes are things that happened. They don't define you. Let them teach you. Then let them go.

5. Don't crave acceptance from others until you've given it to yourself.

6. Accepting your flaws and mistakes doesn't mean you're giving in, it means you're brave enough to keep going and reach for a better future

7. Be proud of your achievements, they were hard won, and if they nearly broke you just know you were strong enough to make it.

8. Don't be afraid to shine - you can be as bright as the sun.

9. Be true to yourself, and you will have no regrets or fears but only a future that has no limits.

10. There's only one person that can make you as happy as you can possibly be, and that's you.

11. You can go wherever your dreams take you, go as far as the limits of your own imagination to the point where you are who you were meant to be.

12. As long as you try your best, you will never lose.

13. If you try to please everyone, you invariably end up pleasing no one, including yourself. Put your happiness first, then look at trying to help others.

14. Make your own happiness the most important part of your day and you will have the strength to shine and spread your light to everyone you see.

15. Take your time to get to know yourself and you'll make a new best friend.

16. Why can't you be more like someone you wish you could be? Because you were made exactly how you were meant to be, which means you're perfect.

17. If you love yourself the rest of the world will fall head over heels for you.

18. If you want more, take it, if you wish for less, shed something, if you long for the world, reach for the sky and touch the stars.

19. It's not the diamonds on your fingers or the latest fashions that make you rich, it's the beauty and strength inside that makes you priceless.

20. You can go as far as your imagination will take you.

21. What looks better on you than a million-dollar necklace? The sparkle in your eye when you know you're worth much more than any diamond.

22. Save an extra big dose of love for the most important person in your life: you!

23. You can't love who you are today without forgiving the person you were yesterday.

24. Whatever anyone else says about you, they can't hurt you anywhere near as much as you can if you listen to them.

25. Self-confidence is the best accessory you can wear.

26. Don't turn your back on the one person who needs you the most: yourself.

27. If you love yourself for who you are, you are loving a one of a kind which is as precious as the rarest diamond.

28. If you see your own flaws and love yourself anyway, you'll be able to love another through good times and bad.

29. Tomorrow is uncertain, yesterday is gone, today is the time to take control of your life. Live in this moment without regret or remorse and make tomorrow a better today.

30. If no one is perfect; we are all imperfectly perfect.

31. If you had to decide whether to love yourself or loathe yourself the choice is easy: love yourself and you'll always be cherished.

32. No one can take away your self-esteem because it's yours, it belongs to you. So, nurture it, grow it, and it will make you unbeatable.

33. Your body is a wonder, your mind is as complex as the universe itself, don't underestimate what you're capable of because you're a miracle.

34. Be as kind to yourself as you are to your best friend, take yourself to lunch, lavish flowers, presents and treats on yourself, be your own Valentine every day.

35. You're not special because someone tells you so. You're special because you are you.

36. Being kind to yourself is as important as breathing. You wouldn't deprive yourself of air, so don't withhold kindness from yourself.

37. You are never alone if you have your own back. You will never be lonely if you listen to your heart.

38. Write a letter to your past self and bury it deep enough that it doesn't haunt you but not so deep that you forget.

39. Without mistakes, getting it right isn't half as rewarding. Without losses, winning wouldn't be such a windfall. Without falling, rising wouldn't be such a triumph.

40. Don't try to figure out what it takes to make someone else happy, do whatever it is that makes you happy and let them join in with the fun.

41. If all you've ever wanted is to be loved; then give the gift of love to yourself.

42. No one can ever know you as well as you know yourself, so be kind to the one who knows you best.

43. There are things about you that people wish they could be. There are things you've done that people wish they could do. If you wish you could be like someone else, remember there are people who wish they could be you.

44. Your strength is in knowing how strong you are.

FINAL WORDS

Learning to love yourself may be one of the most difficult things you'll ever do. It's not just about learning how to love, it is about unlearning a lifetime of behaviors that effectively prevent you from loving yourself. Negative self-talk has such a powerful effect on every aspect of our lives from our self-esteem to our relationships and all of our life choices. We simply can't flourish if we listen to negative self-talk. But as soon as we start to replace negative self-talk by debunking them, replacing them with positivity and controlling our emotions we can completely change the way we think, act and feel.

It's hard not to compare ourselves with celebrities and friends on social media. As you've learned in this book, social media is merely a snapshot of someone's life. Nobody is perfect and the only way to feel better about yourself is to stop comparing.

Failure is a natural part of life, it's how we learn. We don't get annoyed at a toddler for falling down when they take their first step. So, we shouldn't beat ourselves up when we occasionally fall. Remember that failure is a stepping stone to success. Looking forward instead of back will help you manage your expectations about failure and success. You've learned not to dwell on the past or beat yourself up for your previous actions. Live in the moment and look towards a successful future and you will thrive.

You've learned that self-worth isn't about what you own, what you do for a living or what you look like. Self-worth is about *you*. The exercise you completed, listing the things you like about yourself, will hopefully have proven to you that you are worthy. You're worthy of self-love and you deserve to take time out for yourself. As you've seen, denying yourself some "me time" actually makes you less productive at work and in everyday life. So, take that day at the health spa—it will be so good for your mental and physical well-being; plus, you deserve it!

If your work, play and home environments don't make you happy, then you should not settle. Settling will hold you back from your true destiny and prevent you from being as happy as you can be. Instead create environments you can thrive in with a job that makes you feel empowered, a relationship that makes you happy and friends who bring out the best in you.

You may be a "yes person." You don't want to disappoint people. As you've seen in this book, saying no can actually be a good thing, allowing people to appreciate you more and respect your boundaries. Don't put yourself last! You will only succeed if you ensure your own happiness before that of others.

Self-compassion is one of the main ways you can show yourself love. Make sure you live a balanced life that includes "me time" and time spent with loved ones and friends. Nourish your body with healthy comfort food and exercise you enjoy, and you will strike a balance that keeps you on top of your game. Finally, include mindfulness meditation in order to help you improve your focus, control your emotions and feel calm.

You deserve to love yourself. You can achieve your goals with a positive mindset. Use the tools in this book to take action, take risks and achieve the success you've always dreamed of. You don't need to fear your past anymore. The future is yours, and if you can acknowledge the incredible person you are, you will be happy, healthy and successful in whatever you put your mind to!